The Old Roads of England

The Old Roads of England

Sir William Addison

B. T. BATSFORD LTD • LONDON

4

First published 1980
© Sir William Addison 1980
Set in Alphatype Garamond 11 on 13pt by
Modern Text Typesetting, Southend-on-Sea.
Printed and bound in Great Britain by
Morrison & Gibb Ltd., London and Edinburgh
for the publishers B. T. Batsford Ltd,
4 Fitzhardinge Street, London W1H 0AH

ISBN 0 7134 1714 5

Contents

List of Illustrations

LIST OF MAPS

Acknowledgments

The author gratefully acknowledges his indebtedness to Mr Gerald Curtis, who has played a leading part in measures for conservation in Essex in recent years, Mr John Hunter of the Essex County Planning Department, Mr Peter Walne, County Archivist of Hertfordshire, and Mr Bernard Ward, fellow Verderer of Epping Forest for 20 years, for reading this book in MS and making helpful suggestions for amendment.

The author and publishers wish to thank the following for permission to reproduce the photographs included in this book: Aerofilms Ltd (7); Janet and Colin Bord (1, 3, 11, 12, 25, 26); Cambridge University Collection—copyright reserved (2, 6, 8, 13, 16); J. Dixon Scott, F.R.P.S. (5), F. Frith and Co Ltd (34); Fay Godwin's Photo Files (4, 15); London Transport Executive (28); Mary Evans Picture Library (21, 35, 36); Frank Rodgers (14); Olive Smith (33); Reece Winstone (29); Nos. 9, 10, 17, 18, 19, 20, 22, 23, 24, 27, 30, 31, 32 and 37 are from the publishers' collection. The maps were drawn by Mr Bernard Ward.

Introduction

————◆◆◆————

THE IDEA for this book came to me one summer afternoon while lying on soft moorland turf, drowsily tracing the lines of sheep tracks along the steep slopes of an Exmoor valley and of farm-ways worn into the foothills by countless cattle being driven down for milking. Suddenly, while thinking of nothing in particular, I sensed as never before the meaning of the phrase 'The unimaginable touch of Time'.

No doubt a lifetime in which most of the leisure has been spent exploring the English countryside and its records for evidence of local history gave depth to that momentary sensation. One of the pleasant things about growing old is that scenes and events forgotten or set aside for fifty or sixty years return with clarity to mean much more than they meant while they were being experienced. It is natural that this should be so; but we miss the value of it if we fail to recognise how much memory of the past enriches the present. This is particularly true of travel – and not surprisingly so, since highways are to the countryside what arteries are to the body, as we acknowledge by calling them arterial. And we know how usefully the body subconsciously stores up memories to our later advantage. By the same token byways are the veins of the landscape.

For thousands of years man's survival has depended on both highways and byways. What began as animal trails, trodden hard by prehistoric hunters, developed into long-distance trackways, some of which were paved for marching armies and are now 'A' roads. In some parts of the country packhorse trails were paved before roads, and these proliferated into pilgrim ways, market ways, corpse ways, keg ways, drift ways, hog ways, and a score of other local trackways to meet man's real or imaginary needs in hunting, herding, ploughing, worshipping, and trysting long before transport was thought to depend upon wheels.

It must have been in a similarly reflective mood that Robert Louis Stevenson wrote: 'I am told there are people who do not care for maps, and find it hard to believe. The names, the shapes of the woodlands, the courses of the roads and rivers, the prehistoric footsteps of man still distinctly traceable up hill and down dale, the mills and the ruins, the ponds and the ferries, perhaps the *Standing Stone* or the *Druidic Circle* on the heath; here is an inexhaustible fund of interest for any man with eyes to see and twopence-worth of imagination to understand with'. In fact, many of these sources of interest adopted singly have filled the working hours, let alone the leisure, of scholars whose conclusions have been printed in the Proceedings of learned societies, where they have triggered off disputes that have kept correspondence columns going for months, and rival projects for years.

This is not that kind of book. I have read fairly widely in the publications of county historical and archaeological societies in search of answers to questions that have perplexed me; but as one who is by nature an amateur I have never felt any urge to enter these contests, although I have sometimes reached my own unshakeable conclusions! So in writing this book I have aimed at nothing more ambitious than to set down some of the observations on old roads that I have accumulated over the years in diaries, notebooks, and files, as well as in what used to be a fairly good memory, in the hope that younger country-lovers may be helped to find more quickly than I did the answers to questions that all travellers ask, but not all have time to pursue.

Those who are starting out on similar searches today are immeasurably more fortunate than the young of my generation were, because they have W. G. Hoskins to put them on the right track before they get their boots on. I distinctly remember how fascinated I was when I first read *The Making of the English Landscape* more than twenty years ago by the way he could take a single sheet of the Ordnance Survey and find in it every variety of road, from prehistoric trackway to modern bypass. The area chosen for the purpose extended north of Oxford to a few miles beyond Banbury, and from Chipping Norton on the west to a point beyond Brackley on the east. Its main artery was the Jurassic Way – better known as the Fosse Way – which is probably at least four thousand years old, and not only defines parish boundaries but by its varying width provided Professor Hoskins with clues to the dates at which land on either side came into cultivation whilst on the chalk uplands ancient trackways remained practically undisturbed.

It was this last piece of skill in landscape detection that gripped me. I had so often stood on a hilltop from which an industrial town with roads leading up to it could be seen in the distance, yet all around me were immemorial sheep tracks, and rudely reinforced foot-paths that must have been strengthened for some purpose other than the convenience of pedestrians. As a rule they turned out to be packhorse trails; but *The Making of the English Landscape* showed me that what had hitherto been casual observations and scraps of amateur detection could be pieced together in the mind to provide a picture with an extra dimension.

In that same book Professor Hoskins says 'the interest of an inquiry such as this, and one cannot say it too often, lies in the detail of the subject'. It is a view that every topographer must share, knowing from his own personal experience that it is the study of detail that makes the subject what Robert Louis Stevenson called 'An inexhaustible fund of interest'. But alas! whereas the span of a man's life is absurdly short, the lifetime of a road seems never ending.

Perhaps it may be thought that preoccupation with this faculty for survival that roads appear almost uniquely to possess has been the main theme of this book. It has certainly made the map of England for me the most wonderful of all palimpsests. And when Professor Hoskins said that understanding came with the study of detail I realised that this was a subject on which everyone – to quote Stevenson again – 'with eyes to see and twopence-worth of imagination to understand with', had something to contribute.

In my books *Understanding English Place Names* and *Understanding English Surnames** I have tried to encourage a 'do-it-yourself' approach to those subjects. I want

*Batsford, 1978

to do the same here by relating what I have found and followed up by study in those parts of the country that I know reasonably well, in order to show what others may do in their bit of countryside. That is why, although I have tried to do enough research to make this a semi-serious study of the development of our roadway system I have kept it to some extent personal. It may be thought that this has resulted in my falling between two stools. If that has happened I can only say 'So be it'. I stand by the belief that roads are both to be experienced and read about, and that either is inadequate for full understanding without the other.

My personal experiences are scattered throughout the chapters of this book; but as an illustration of how one man's observations can stimulate another's, I remember that when I followed Professor Hoskins in his progress of interpretation along his chosen length of the Fosse Way, my mind immediately took up the challenge in relation to the through-way that in those days I knew best, the Great North Road. I knew, of course, that as the Fosse Way had been deviated – although only to a minor extent – so Ermine Street had been deviated to form the Old North Road, which in turn was deviated when coaches replaced waggons to its historic line as a great coaching road figuring in a host of novels as well as in accounts of travel. But I hadn't then fully appreciated the inevitability of maintaining its course across Yorkshire through every vicissitude, simply because it was only by crossing the mouth of every dale in succession that access could be gained to the countryside that produced metal before the Romans came, wool when the Cistercians made the fells one vast sheep walk, and the products of cottage industries later in all the dale villages. Nor did I then fully appreciate how much we can learn about the modifications we observe in the landscape we drive through from the names of the villages, which along the Great North Road record Saxon, Anglian, Danish, Norse, and Celtic settlement. No-one can fail to be impressed by the massive bridges that span the rivers pouring down from the Pennines; but only by knowing something of place-name origins can we see the significance of the river-names that strong-wristed masons – and Yorkshire was famous for them – had carved into the parapets. And now, in the interests of soul-destroying speed, this great highway has again been deviated to bypass the very towns and villages it was created and re-created to sustain.

I have no love myself for concrete motorways running under concrete bridges to reach one concrete jungle from another; but if they can siphon off the speed-hogs and juggernauts I am ready to applaud their extension. They may help us to discover belatedly what a valuable part of our heritage our old roads are, and how much more interesting the names and buildings of the villages we drive through are than those giant hoardings along our motorways recording the diminishing distances to destinations that no man who really understands what life is about would want to reach anyway!

It may be thought an odd commentary on progress that 50 years ago few would have needed to be convinced of the interest that travel in a country as small as ours can provide. In those pre-precast concrete days a journey of 50 miles was an adventure and every object along its course was noticed. However, while universal mobility has killed off much of the novelty of travel, it has extended its range of experience. If we keep to the old roads, we are all able now to discover variations of landscape and buildings on a scale unknown to more than a privileged few in former generations. So there is gain as well as loss, and having suffered the loss we need to be all the more vigilant in safeguard-ing the gain. I don't know how inevitable some of the losses along our country roads were. I personally was very attached to the gravel surfacing of our tarmacadamed byways in Essex. It sparkled in the sun, blended pleasingly with the green of grass verges, and at night caught the light from either the moon or a car's headlamps better than the grey abomination that has succeeded it. When I say so I am fobbed off with scientific jargon and that administrator's trump card: 'It is done in the interests of road safety', although I have never been able to see the evidence for this, and it still strikes me as the kind of card that a conjuror produces from his sleeve.

But if we are losing distinctively local roadways, we still have local styles in walling, hedging, and ditching that reflect the material traditionally available to those who first constructed them, and the wealth or poverty of those who met the cost when financing was still local. There is now at least as much detail to be deciphered in the material that fringes the road as in the carriageway itself. There are granite walls in Cornwall that mark prehistoric boundaries of estates, and we now know that some of the deep lanes that appear to gouge their way through the foothills of Dartmoor began as double-ditches delved in Saxon times to mark similar boundaries. The soil thrown up in the process has now consolidated into massive embankments, with tangled roots gripping the soil like fingers clinging to a cliff face. Some of the other roads that began as boundary lines were originally baulks separating cultivated furlongs, and the soil thrown up when these were widened now forms the lower banks capped by hedgerows that we see along the valley roads. My botanist friends tell me that there is a known succession of plants to be identified along the hedges and grass verges of these roads which enables their age to be determined. The hawthorn itself, which takes its name from words meaning 'hedge-thorn', is a native, and present-day hedgerows in regions enclosed early may be descended from sprigs poked into the dike in Saxon times. Its flower gave rise to the popular saying: 'Cast not a clout till May be out', which refers to the plant not the month, and com-memorates its association with May Day festivals. I am told that ash will develop under hawthorn, followed by field-maple, which appears to be characteristic of medieval hedges.

In stone country walls are equally revealing records of the past and of the comparative wealth of the local community. An interesting tour could be devised studying these alone, tracing them from Dorset through the Cotswolds and Derbyshire to Cumbria. In the well-to-do Cotswolds they are neatly built of flat honey-coloured stones in orderly layers, capped with uprights. In Oxfordshire we see them round great estates, most notably round Blenheim, and even along farm walls. In the Pennines they are built of irregular rough-hewn stones blasted out of the rock in fellside quarries, which neverthe-less conform strictly to the traditional pattern described by Arthur Raistrick in one of the Dalesman Pocket Books. Practically all were capped with a row of coping stones; but in parts of Weardale a row of sods was built in at the top, in the belief that this would bond the stones together and keep out the water – just as in Devon cob walls were thatched. In the limestone belt of Craven in Yorkshire the walls may be full of fossils, bearing evidence to the sea having washed over the region before the land took its present form.

If the main stream of commercial traffic can be taken off such roads as these, we may ask with some hope of getting the right answer whether the time has come for efforts to be made on a national scale for preserving parts at least of our ancient roadway system, both for amenity and for their value as records in the history of travel and transport that can be followed without a break for a period of up to four thousand years or more. But if we get the right answer, we shall still have to bear in mind that when the public acquire the freedom to enjoy a landscape they also acquire the freedom to destroy it.

CHAPTER ONE

Ancient Trackways

————◆•••◆————

IN PREHISTORIC TIMES the familiar well-groomed landscape of Southern England, with its 'best kept villages' and fertile water meadows, was a vast morass from Somerset in the West to Kent and Essex in the East, with woodland and tangled scrub above the flood plain. The rivers had not then worn the deep beds that now enable them to drain away the water running down from the chalk ridges – the 'bold majestic downs' that sprawl across the entire region in lonely wind-swept nonchalance no matter what goes on in the valleys between them. Only these can now give us the feel of the original terrain across which wild beasts and the hunters who stalked them trod out tracks that skirted the bogs and scaled the heights as they moved from one browsing ground to another. To both man and beast these tracks would become as clearly marked as if they had been sign-posted, and every experienced hunter would know where his prey would be found, not only at every season of the year but at every hour of the day. They belonged to a way of life regulated only by the sun and the seasons, which continued for thousands of years in Britain, and is still followed in Africa and Asia.

Some of these prehistoric trackways would be much longer than might be expected. The grass available in Neolithic times would be sparse by comparison with that to be found today on either the moors of the South-West of England or the fells of the North; but the range of the tracks would still be restricted to what was required to meet the domestic needs of primitive life, of which salt would be one. The first long-distance tracks would come when the hunter became a husbandman and needed tools. He would already have discovered the value of the flints he could poke out of the downland chalk for use as arrow-heads, scrapers, and prickers; but when it came to felling trees he needed stones large enough to be fashioned into axe-heads, and as these were not to hand every-where flint-ways were established along with saltways as the first of the community-ways that continue to score our hillsides, many because they continued in use as packhorse trails until well into the nineteenth century.

Flint quarries with shafts open for inspection can still be seen at Grimes Graves near Brandon on the Norfolk-Suffolk boundary, in which antler-picks for scraping out the flints have been found. There must have been thousands of such workings over the country as a whole. They were our first factories. More than a hundred have been plotted at Martin's Clump, Over Wallop, near Salisbury in Wiltshire,* and more than two hundred at Cissbury and elsewhere on the Sussex Downs. Each of these workings

*Proc. Hants. Field Club and Arch. Soc., vol. XII (1934)

acquired its network of tracks, and they would have provided valuable evidence of local settlement of density or sparseness of population if most of them had not become overgrown with turf or lost under metalled roads. Fortunately, burrowing rabbits often put us on the scent of them, and we have direct clues to their distribution areas in cases where quarries became known for their distinctive stone. A particular blue-black flint, for example, that was widely used for arrow-heads and scrapers came from quarries in Devon west of Totnes, and others at Beer. Greenstone for axe-heads came from several quarries in Cornwall. The wide distribution of both is explained by the ease with which they could be carried by water from ports with sea-links at the mouth of the Avon, and from there to Salisbury Plain, with its ancient routes across the Cotswolds or the Marlborough Downs to the Midlands or the East of England.

In the South-East, flint from the Sussex Downs provided axe-heads for tree felling in Kent from Neolithic times, and the North of England came into the market early through the discovery that the hardest stone for polishing into sharp blades was the crystalline rock of the Langdale Pikes in the Lake District. No doubt the axe factory at Great Langdale explains the early cultivation of many small clearings in the North-West. Judging by the tracks that converge on them, and the quality of their stone, the Langdale quarries must have been the most famous in the North and this makes it reasonable to believe that many Lakeland tracks began as flint-ways.

Place-name evidence for flint-ways is rare; but we have it for the early popularity of stone from the North for use as millstones. Quernmore, near Lancaster, means the moor where millstones were quarried, and Quarndon in Derbyshire the hill from which they were quarried. So from one source or another we have abundant evidence that the northern fells supported a community of Bronze Age farmers, cultivating small plots of stony ground comparable with the lynchets along the Berkshire and Sussex downs and ridgeways, where early tillers of the soil discovered that the combination of clay and limestone produces a fertile soil.

When men began to travel such long distances as from the extreme west to the extreme north of England to obtain tools and machinery for grinding grain into flour, and later to barter and trade, it was found that the only safe tracks were along the watersheds. The re-opening of the most historic of these ridgeways for long-distance footpaths has been the most exciting thing that has happened to country-lovers for a long time. Throughout most of their length these first through-ways, which were always clear of woodland apart from the odd brake of thorn or a few scattered juniper trees, were in use at least 4,000 years ago. On the Continent they have been established for the long-distance transport of precious metals much earlier, and it was the discovery of metal in the South-West of England that brought ridgeways into use as trade-routes here.

The first tin-and lead-ways, like the first flint-ways, led only to ports from which the metal could be shipped; but as trade expanded land-routes were developed from that hub of the great wheel of trackways which now staggers the mind by the splendour of its isolation and symbolic power: Stonehenge, the one stupendously impressive monument to a culture that was already coming to its end when the Bronze Age culture began.

The vast and well-drained plateau of Salisbury Plain was ready-made by Nature for the purpose of long-distance transport in its early stages. As soon as the heights were scaled,

1 *The Ridgeway where it passes 'Wayland's Smithy'*

2 *The Icknield Way, running north-east from the Chiltern Escarpment*

long bare ridges were seen to run east and west, with shorter ones running north and
south. When these were explored an eastern route was found to run to the chalk cliffs of
Dover, and a westward one to the mines of Cornwall, to which Phoenician traders were
already bringing precious stones to barter for lead and tin. All these long-distance tracks
sent out branches; but the main trunk ridgeway eastwards was the Wiltshire-Berkshire
trackway that crossed the Thames at Streatley to run through the Goring Gap and along
the Chiltern foothills where it became known as the Upper Icknield Way. After crossing
what are now the counties of Hertfordshire and Cambridgeshire it continued to Ickling-
ham, between Bury St Edmunds and Mildenhall, and finally reached the East Anglian
coast at the Wash. The Lower Icknield Way is now a metalled road at its western end.
The main long-distance ridgeway westward divided early to send out a branch to north
Devon, with breaks in Somerset, while a ridgeway across the Cotswolds was to prove of
ever increasing importance and to develop eventually into a ridgeway complex.

All these ridgeways are signposted, as it were, by barrows that cover the burial
chambers of tribal chieftains. There are so many of them in Wiltshire that Salisbury
Plain has been described as one vast cemetery. Even on Dartmoor, 24 of the 38 stone
avenues lead to barrows. Some of the old clapper bridges, of which the best surviving
example is at Postbridge – an important town for tinners – are impressive reminders of
that vanished way of life which in course of time became so highly organised that at its
peak ingots of tin were carried daily to the stannary towns of Plympton, Tavistock,
Ashburton and Chagford to be assayed and stamped. All these places are reached today
by motor roads that began as trails for the sturdy packhorses bred on the Moor, called
widge-beasts. Lord Widgery's surname is a corruption of Widge- or Wedgeworthy. A
'worthy' was an enclosure, and the first part of the name refers to the fenced funnel,
which was like a duck decoy in that it was wide at the open end so that the wild moorland
ponies could be driven into it. Master Widgery was in charge of the enclosure; the men
who made the fences were called widgers, or wedgers.

Many of the old clapper bridges on the Moor have been rebuilt several times after
being carried away by flood water. Tarr Steps, to my knowledge, has been rebuilt three

3 Clapperbridge over the East Dart at Postbridge, Dartmoor

times within the present century. It is doubtful whether any of them are ancient in the sense of being prehistoric. Their name, at all events, is derived from *claperius,* and so is Roman.

The great obstacle to establishing a through-route westward on dry land was the need to cross the swamps of the Somerset Levels, and nothing in the entire history of ancient trackways is to me more remarkable than the way in which this was achieved more than four thousand years ago. Somerset derives its name from being 'the land of the summer dwellers'. Many of its place-names end in -ey, signifying that they were formerly islands. The Poldens in the north of the county have a name that means hills surrounded by pools. Their ridgeway has Sedgemoor, 'the marsh where the sedge grows', on one side and the Isle of Avalon on the other. These names are themselves clues to the immensity of the problem that confronted those who built the recently discovered timber trackway across the Shapwick-Meare marsh to enable travellers to reach the Polden ridge from the river Brue at the time when the bogs were beginning to dry out. This prehistoric causeway was constructed of hazel and birch branches laid longitudinally, with brushwood transversely across them, supported in places by stakes driven into the peat. Radiocarbon analysis has dated this trackway to the third millenium BC*

These first marshland causeways were superseded in the first millenium BC by 'corduroy roads', formed by the reversed process of laying stout timbers on a brushwood foundation, a method that continued in use for thousands of years in forestry work.

The long-distance footpaths established under the National Parks and Access to the Countryside Act 1949 have been described by experts for use by ramblers in admirable official publications; but motorists need not feel deterred. A short walk from a car parked as near to a moorland summit as can be reached by road will often bring the surrounding countryside into focus, particularly if the motorist has had his eyes open while travelling to his chosen point. Each country lover will have his own favourite region. One of mine, as may have been gathered, is Exmoor, which is especially good because much of its border was enclosed late and all its main roads follow the routes of ancient trackways. Approaching the Moor from Devon, the ridgeway from Morte Point to Wood Barrow can be followed as far as Blackmoor Gate, and one from Wood Barrow to Sandyway Cross along the boundary between Somerset and Devon. There are other ridgeways running to Bampton and half a dozen other places where ancient routes cross. But the best of all the Exmoor ridgeways from the motorists' point of view is the one that runs either along or close to the A39 road between Porlock and Lynmouth, which no-one could ever imagine was planned for motorists. Its conformity with the old ridgeway is shown by the way its course is marked out by round barrows and the steepness of its descents into Lynmouth and Porlock, which provided hair-raising experiences in coaching days, although when the last of the 'Tony Wellers' took his first railway journey from Minehead to Taunton he said he felt safer on his own box seat!

From Porlock the old ridgeway climbed Bossington Hill, which must have outporlocked Porlock, and continued to Minehead along the five miles of the 'Scenic Road', again marked by round barrows, past Selworthy Beacon to descend into Minehead at the

*Proc. of the Prehistoric Soc.: New Series, vol. XXVI

significantly named Holloway Street, a name that will be dealt with presently. From Minehead it continued inland by way of Alcombe to Dunster (named Torr in Domesday), down Mill Lane and over the Brendon Hills to Winsford.

The reference to the river Brue being used to reach a convenient point on Shapwick Heath to attempt a crossing of the marsh to the safety of the Polden Ridge may remind us that in undrained country the safest passage through valleys was by water, and that while the land was drying out rivers and roads were combined for through-routes as they still are in the jungle. In any case, running water must always have been man's best compass after sunset. A Dartmoor man recently said to me that he could never understand how anyone could get lost on the Moor. A short walk, he argued, would bring him within sound of running water wherever he might be, and as water runs downhill it could not fail to bring him to either a village or a farmstead. A mist was blowing up at the time and I confess that I did not find his argument convincing – nor, I suspect, would he if snow had been falling. Nevertheless, the riverside tracks that are now minor but well-surfaced roads down the narrow valleys of the Barle and the Exe in the West Country, and the Derbyshire and Yorkshire dales in the North, must all follow ancient trackways linked to ridgeways. I remember being struck by the way they run down to Kettlewell in Wharfedale. In the East of England, although often obliterated by either intensive agriculture or industry, they are still to be found, as we should expect them to be, since river routes were used almost exclusively for penetration into the country by early tribal invaders. An important Iron Age trade route, with camps of that period along its course, ran up the Lea Valley from the Thames, to continue up the Stort and link up with the Icknield Way. In lowland country the extent to which rivers were used for transport explains the frustrating local-road systems, so frequently found near rivers, that come to dead-ends at river-banks.

The importance of barrows in signposting ridgeways is best seen in Wiltshire. There is a point from which a remarkable line of them can be reached from the road that passes close to Stonehenge. It is where the A303 intersects the A360 running north from Salisbury. A trackway can be reached without much exertion from this point that has 26 barrows of seven different types near it. Cranborne Chase, which formerly extended west of the Avon from Ringwood to Salisbury, is probably the best extended area for exploring earth evidence of this kind. Long barrows were like modern vaults in that they were opened up for succeeding burials in chieftain families. Some of them well merit their name. A long barrow near the Winterbourne Stoke crossroads is 240 ft long, and the long barrow at Pimperne, alongside the A354 road through Dorset is even longer. Round barrows are much more numerous. Most of them date from the Bronze Age and hundreds can be spotted along the South Downs Way as it runs towards Eastbourne.

There are two main concentrations of ancient burial sites: one extending from Salisbury Plain to the Cotswolds, the other on the Yorkshire Wolds. Other concentrations are found on the Lincolnshire Wolds and in the Peak District of Derbyshire. One of the most remarkable memorials to be found anywhere is at Rudston in East Yorkshire, which takes its name from a monolith, or 'rood stone', near the church, which has two long barrows side by side. Circular prehistoric enclosures, surrounded by ditch and bank on the same design as Stonehenge, and also called 'henges', are found in Derbyshire and the North Riding of Yorkshire. There are six of them within seven miles of Ripon, and isolated circles in several of the Yorkshire dales. To the west of these, Bronze Age hut foundations are found over the whole of the limestone region of Craven and south Westmorland.

Several northern prehistoric trackways will be more usefully referred to when we look at packhorse trails and drove roads; but they cannot all be left until later. The Pass of Stainmore, for example, was a trade route along which copper and gold ornaments were carried into Yorkshire from the Lake District and Ireland as early as 1500 BC, as we know from the bronze and stone axe-heads found in round barrows at Dalton, and a gold bracelet found at Greta Bridge. Another northern ridgeway that figured for thousands of years in early history was the one that follows the ridge between the Derwent and the Dove, passing close to Arbor Low, the third largest stone circle in England, which dates from between 2000 and 1800 BC. Two thousand years later this prehistoric trackway became the Roman road to Buxton. So magnificent are the views from points on these Derbyshire ridgeways that it is not surprising that Tom Stephenson started the first and finest of the long-distance footpaths, the Pennine Way, from the Peak.

All these mountain passes are associated with Iron Age camps, or hill-forts, of the half-millenium BC, which are usually shown on maps as 'rings' or 'castles'. They are often found to encircle the tops of hills which would provide views of the approach of an enemy. Later, when defence was not the prime concern, their prominence served the contrary purpose of being places that could be seen from a distance, and they came into use as assembly points for great sheep and cattle fairs, particularly where they were near the crossings of green lanes where caravans of traders could arrange to meet and barter silver, tin, or lead, for horses, sheep, or goats.

Contemporary with the barrows and the hill-camps, but rarer than either, are the causeway-camps found on the chalk downs of the South of England. These are always connected with ancient trackways and were probably used by people travelling to the flint quarries. The fact that the word 'knap' in Knap Hill is found on the map at the point where the ridgeway from the Marlborough Downs to Alton Barnes drops into the Vale of Pewsey after crossing Wansdyke is significant, and the place itself is an outstanding example of a hill top encircled by a causeway-camp. Its long-barrow, formerly known as Woden's Barrow, is now known as Adam's Grave. Alongside it at a lower level is the site of a Romano-British farmstead.

These camps belong to the period when the people who cultivated the valleys between the ridges were still subject to the ravages of tribal warfare. They were constructed as places of safety for cattle and personal possessions with tracks leading up to them called 'ditches'. We have one such track in Epping Forest leading from an Iron Age camp called Ambresbury Banks to what were formerly the water meadows of the Roding Valley. Hampshire has several similar tracks leading from high ground to low. Their generic name is hollow ways, with Holloway, London, the most familiar, if not for the original reason, which was that it was a track worn to a ditch by the passage of cattle between Highgate and Islington. Holloway Street at Minehead is another good example.

The original hollow ways were undoubtedly made by the rain washing away the soil loosened by the hooves of cattle as they scrambled up the slopes to reach their place of safety. Gilbert White describes them perfectly in *The Natural History of Selborne*: 'These roads, running through the malm lands, are, by the traffick of ages, and the fretting of water, worn down through the first stratum of our freestone, and partly through the second; so that they look more like water-courses than roads; and are bedded with naked rag for furlongs together. In many places they are reduced sixteen or eighteen feet beneath the level of the fields; and after floods, and in frosts, exhibit very grotesque and wild appearances, from the tangled roots that are twisted among the strata, and from the torrents rushing down their broken sides'.

While the only available through-routes were along ridgeways it was inevitable that settlements should spring up at key points, most of which were where the rivers had to be forded, since these would be the only points with both a water supply adequate to serve a community and the certainty of trade from travellers obliged to use the ford in order to continue their journey along the next ridgeway. This explains why so many of our historic towns have names ending in 'ford' not 'bridge'. Most of them predate the bridge towns. But while the ford towns grew and prospered over the centuries, the importance of the ridgeways diminished as the forests were felled and the marshes drained to bring more land into cultivation for the support of expanding communities. So today few of our most historic ridgeways can be traced throughout their course, despite the fact that right up to the coming of the railways many of them remained in use as drove roads.

While many important towns owe their rise to their siting at the points where rivers cross ridgeways, there are now few settlements of any size on the actual ridges. These developed secondary roads called summerways because they came into use during dry seasons when travellers were able to reach fords and bridges by less arduous routes. Summerways were terraced in the slopes, usually the southern slopes, of the ridges, following lines roughly parallel with those on the ridges above them. Most of the important ridgeways acquired their summerways, many of which were metalled by the Romans and continue in use as 'B' roads, threading their way through our most attractive villages and small market towns. They are the roads from which we get the best views of our most typically English landscapes, and if we think of it, most of our favourite picnic spots are close to summerways. These hillside roads were found to be convenient for settlement because they were both above the flood level of the valleys and below the wind-blown hilltops, where the springs dried up in summer and the snows lay deep in winter. Outstanding examples of settlements along summerways, which might now be more appropriately called village ways, are found in the Cotswolds, where most of the villages are at middle level. Practically all are between the 500 ft and 750 ft contours. Few are above that level, fewer below it.

In broad terms, the story of roads might be told as reflecting man's progress from barbarism to civilisation, with ancient trackways remaining to a quite amazing degree the permanent framework; but if this were done it would prove to be much less true of secondary than of primary roads. The reason for this is that secondary roads belong to rural rather than urban history, and rural history cannot be cut up and packaged into reigns, or even centuries, in the way urban history can. We may generalise by saying that the nomadic way of life was succeeded by the pastoral, and the pastoral by the agricultural; but the over-riding truth is that in the country Nature rules and all the basic ways of life continue together, with regional modifications dictated by climate and soil. Stock-rearing with animals tethered, we are told, was introduced into England in the third millenium BC. In the West and North of England stock-rearing continues to be basic, whereas in the East and South, once the valleys had been drained and the woodland cleared the land could be brought into intensive cultivation and agriculture could become as scientific as any other industry.

The relevance of this for the support of a large population is reflected in the distribution of our most prosperous cities and the roads that link them to each other and to the Capital. This will be seen when we look at coach roads; but it was already a dominant factor in the century before the Roman invasion. The first stage was reached when the semi-nomadic tribesmen noticed that the grass that grew in some of the more fertile valleys was so abundant that it could be harvested for winter fodder. After the discovery of the use of hay for beasts would come the discovery of corn for men, and it was this discovery that was so vigorously exploited by the Belgic tribes who invaded Kent in the first century BC and spread themselves over Hertfordshire and Essex, establishing the two ancient capitals that became St Albans (Verulamium) and Colchester (Camulodunum). It was undoubtedly because these Belgic tribes had developed the harvesting of corn on such a large scale in these eastern parts that the Roman army marched so quickly through Kent in AD43 and took possession of their capitals. Nowhere else could they have found sufficient food for the legions in so short a time. In most parts of England the people were still living on the milk and flesh produced by their small herds, with no surplus available for either friend or foe.

The effect of the Roman invasion of our roads system was so revolutionary that it has tended to obscure the significance both of what went before and what followed. The Romans had power, wealth and labour at their command. They used them to the limit; but it is still worth pointing out that the Romans started with a natural framework of ancient trackways that had served prehistoric man for more than two thousand years before they came. This framework was the four Great Roads, all of which may well date back to the Early Bronze Age. They were:

1   The North Downs Ridgeway, which extends from Canterbury to Stonehenge, and drew traffic from all the ports of Kent before proceeding on its long course along the Hog's Back into Hampshire north of Andover, and by way of Weyhill to Amesbury and Stonehenge. What is now called the Pilgrims' Way appears to have been its summerway through Kent and Surrey; but on entering Hampshire it became known as the Harroway, which some scholars now suggest may be derived from the Old English *hearg-weg,* 'shrine way', since its destination was Stonehenge long before pilgrims had any interest in Canterbury. Much of the Harroway is now metalled road, but of 'B' rather than 'A' status. On the Basingstoke bypass there is a signpost to 'the Harrow Way', directing travellers to a route which passes Polecat Corner and runs to Kite Hill.

2   The South Downs Ridgeway from Beachy Head to Old Winchester, which runs through a region thickly populated in prehistoric times. The new South Downs Way is deflected from the true route to take in Cissbury and Chanctonbury Rings.

3   The Icknield Way, running from Wessex to the Wash, with the Uffington White Horse alongside it – the only fully-authenticated Iron Age example of this form of art in

4 The North Downs Ridgeway through Berkshire

Britain. On the Wiltshire downs the two main ridgeways are not everywhere distinguish-able. Through Berkshire the Icknield Way runs roughly in line with the North Downs Ridgeway, and after crossing the Thames continues east to Norfolk, to be joined at Thetford by roads from East Anglian ports in the way the North Downs Ridgeway was joined at Canterbury by roads from the Kentish ports. The width of the grass verges along much of the course of the Icknield Way shows that it was kept open for centuries as a drove road.

4   The Fosse Way ran from Axminster in Devon to Lincoln and the Humber, a distance of 182 miles, and nowhere does it deviate more than six miles from the straight line drawn from end to end. As it was so valuable for trade with Northern Europe it may be thought surprising that its course has never been adopted for an arterial road. To appreciate the importance of its contribution to our cultural heritage we only need to be reminded of its association with scores of beautiful villages in the Cotswolds and along its entire course, as well as with the colleges of Oxford. Its more impressive name, the Jurassic Way, is derived from its geological association with the stone of the Jura mountains, exploited in the Bath and Barnack quarries.

5 The Icknield Way near Blewbury, Berkshire

All four Great Roads converged on Salisbury Plain, with its long established links with the Wessex ports, from which in about the year 50 BC the Belgae had followed up their landing in Kent of thirty years earlier to bring to Hampshire and Wiltshire a pre-Roman culture comparable with that in the South-East. This meant that at the end of the period in which our ancient trackways may be considered independently, as at the beginning, Salisbury Plain was firmly established as the hub of the system. Consequently, the two cities of Winchester and Canterbury were already perfectly sited to play the great parts they were destined to play in our national life: Winchester as the capital of the Saxon kings, Canterbury as the ecclesiastical metropolis.

CHAPTER TWO

Roman Roads

❧━━━◆◆◆◆◆━━━❧

THE ROMANS were in Britain for three hundred and fifty years, yet despite the splendour of their public buildings and the enlightenment of their art and culture, the surviving parts of the thousands of miles of roads constructed under their rule are their greatest material monument. And the odd thing about these is that we know so few of them by their Roman names. Watling Street, much of which is incorporated in our London to Holyhead road, takes its name from a tribe that had St Albans as its capital; Ermine Street, the forerunner of the Great North Road, probably takes its name from Earna, the source of Arrington and Armingford. It is, in fact, one of the mysteries of place-names in general that so few of them are Roman. Many of the -chesters have Saxon prefixes.

One irony of this is that of the ancient long-distance roads the one that still bears a Roman name, the Fosse Way, has failed to survive as a trunk road despite its immense historical and amenity importance. Much of the Warwickshire section is now a grass-grown track. The *foss* or ditch, was constructed alongside the roadway as a temporary frontier for the Roman army after completing the occupation of southern England, which was accomplished within four years of the Claudian landing. In developing Ciren-cester as a military post and the capital of a region extending over the Cotswolds, the Romans made it plain that they intended to exploit as well as subdue Britain. Ultimately the roadway coverage was so complete that if Devon and Cornwall are excluded there are few places in England more than twelve miles away from a Roman road, illustrating the truth of Seneca's comment: 'Wheresoever the Roman conquers he inhabits'. It was con-sistent with the Roman character that within so short a time our new masters should have brought into operation their plans as colonists as well as their plans as conquerors, even to the extent of showing what they intended to leave out as well as what they intended to include. Exeter remained the most westerly town to come under their control directly, no doubt because the export of tin from Cornwall practically ceased when sources were found nearer the Mediterranean markets.

Fortunately, the route of the Fosse can be confirmed from a point near South Pether-ton in Somerset to Lincoln – partly because several place-names along its course incor-porate 'Fosse', although most of these are now on 'B' roads. The best evidence, however, is in manorial records, especially Saxon charters. These show that from Cirencester to Bath the road was used for 22 miles continuously to define parish boundaries, and that county boundaries were related to it at such points as the Three Shires Stones, where Gloucester, Somerset and Wiltshire meet, and the Four Shires Stones near Stow-on-the-Wold. Rycknield Street broke off it near Bourton-on-the-Water to run north-west to

Map 1   Main roads in Roman Britain

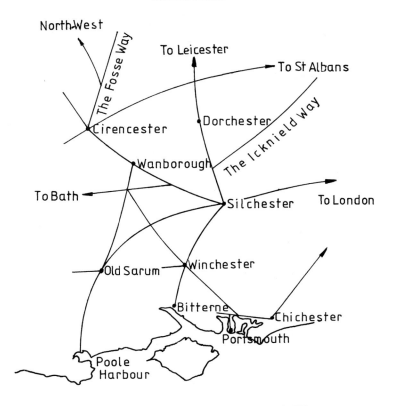

Map 2   Roman roads in the South-West

Wall in Staffordshire by way of the site of Birmingham, then north-eastward to Derby and Chesterfield, to reach Ermine Street near Doncaster.

The reason why the Fosse Way did not become an arterial road throughout its course is obviously that on landing in AD 43 the legions had to use the existing roads, which, while providing for deeper penetration into the country than might have been expected, kept either to the ridgeways or the summerways below them. G. B. Grundy invented the term 'romanised road' for these highways that were adopted by the Romans for incorporation into their roadway system and subjected to extensive straightening and surfacing. The Worcester-Tewkesbury ridgeway is one of them.

It must have been clear from the beginning of the Occupation that of the Four Great Ways of prehistoric origin the one that offered the greatest scope for future development after the Fosse Way was the North Downs Ridgeway. Like the Fosse it crossed country that was already populated and cultivated. So to colonise the region bordering this second romanised road Silchester was developed as a new junction town in the way Cirencester was developed on the Fosse. It was equally strategic. Besides having impressive pre-Roman earthworks enclosing 200 acres, it was near ancient trackways, some of which would have been used by the Belgae in cultivating this rich agricultural region, and one of which linked up with the Berkshire Ridgeway.

In enlarging these existing settlements it must have become increasingly apparent that colonisation would depend upon the draining of the marshes and the felling of woodland in valleys too remote from the ridgeways radiating from Salisbury Plain to be organised from them. A new centre that would be convenient for the country as a whole and for communication with the Continent must be found. Winchester was as too far west as Colchester was too far east and Canterbury too far south.

In seeking the best site for a new capital city the Roman surveyors must have been gratified to find that England as a whole could be divided naturally into two sections, and that the Fosse Way, running diagonally across the country was an existing corridor between the two. To the north and west lay the mountains, at that time sparsely populated, to the south and east lowlands that already had ports linking them with the Continent. The Romans knew that they needed both these two basic divisions. They must send prospectors into the hills in search of the mineral wealth that had been one of their objectives in landing, and they must teach the people in the lowlands new skills in husbandry. Above all, the new national capital must be conveniently placed for exporting from the whole of Britain. In short, it must be chosen in relation to what amounted to a Roman forerunner of the Common Market. To this multiple question London was the obviously answer in the first century as it has been ever since.

The military road system—that is to say, the system for the movement of troops and the subjugation of the population—was practically completed by the end of the first century AD; but it was inevitably an uneven operation. The Belgic tribes inhabiting the South-East had come from the Marne Valley and were people with an advanced way of life, who were obviously able to come to terms with the Romans better than were the Celts in the West of England, who immediately took to the hills, and there continued the guerilla warfare that made them the individualists and rebels they still are. Apart from this lack of racial sympathy the Celts had little at stake. As hunters and pastoral people they could drive their flocks and small herds into the hills at the first sign of an enemy approaching, unlike the Belgae, who had valuable crops in holdings cultivated with heavier ploughs than those used in backward regions. Perhaps the clearest evidence of the friendly relationship established between the natives and the invaders is in the close proximity of the pre-Roman and post-Roman settlements at the two Belgic capitals, Camulodunum and Verulamium. Although Colchester was seen to be too far east for a national capital, its citizens were so friendly that even when London was established as the capital, the triangle formed by London, Colchester, and St Albans became the base for the conquest of the whole of the region directly to the north of it.

The conquest of the North of England came 30 to 40 years later than the conquest of the area south of the Fosse frontier, along which a protective line of forts was built. In AD71 the legions pressed north from these fortresses to Chester, and from that great stronghold constructed three roads: one through Manchester to York, another from Manchester through the Forest of Bowland to Kirkby Lonsdale, and a third through Warrington and Wigan to Lancaster, with the object of bringing the whole of northern England into subjection in one concerted drive from the five bases of Chester, Manchester, Ribchester, Lancaster and York.

Progress turned out to be so slow that it was not until about AD80 that Agricola built the Stane Gate (stone road) that runs for nearly 40 miles from Carlisle to Corbridge, and not until 40 years later again that Hadrian's Wall was built to the north of that. Despite the impressive list of Roman remains discovered in the North, where historical and archaeological interest has always been strong, the fact is that 80% of our Romanised towns lie south of the line from the Severn Estuary to the Wash, which means south of the Fosse. Consequently the roads of the south-east of England and the south Midlands can best be studied for civil administration, those of the North for military control exercised from forts that were satellites of York and Chester. No such forts were needed in the lowlands of the South until the military defence of the Saxon Shore became necessary so much later. Nevertheless, in the lowlands of the North, such as the Plain of York, no less than in those of the South, the occupation became complete – so much so, that nowhere was the Romanisation of civil government more absolute than at York itself.

Such domination of the North could only have been achieved and maintained by local control, to which Hadrian's Wall is so impressive a monument. So although the natives of the North never accepted Roman culture in the way they were later to accept Anglian and Scandinavian, there are many mementoes of happy co-existence, like that of the inscription on a fine tombstone in the museum at South Shields to the memory of the British wife of a Syrian from Palmyra who had settled in Northumberland.

As colonisation advanced in the South the ramparts of the Roman fortresses on the Fosse frontier became city walls, the praetorium a market square, and the through-ways that had been strengthened for military purposes were expanded into networks of minor roads radiating from such places as Gloucester and Cirencester. Many junctions on the pre-Roman trackway system became administrative centres under Rome, while some, for no apparent reason, either decayed or failed to develop. One of these, surely, in the region with which I am most familiar is Braughing, a Hertfordshire village in an entirely rural environment at the convergence of four roads, and near both Ermine Street and the Roman road across Hertfordshire to Great Chesterford in north-west Essex, where it linked up with the Icknield Way. The present village is slightly away from the Roman settlement, which is not an uncommon feature in this part of the country, and on the credit side it should be added that it did become the head of a Hundred and an ecclesiastical deanery.

There must be many places like Braughing, and often the explanation of their failure to develop must be that long stretches of road used for rapid conquest were abandoned and the settlements along their course allowed to decay with them. A major example is the Portway (market-way) between Silchester and Andover, which failed to maintain its early importance. O. G. S. Crawford* argues persuasively that the fact that a road which is known to be ancient is straight does not prove that it has continued in use since Roman times. He even suggests that straightness might be evidence against continuous use since roads known to have been used over long periods are inclined to 'wobble' in places, and he instances the road from Canterbury to London via Rochester, and Akeman Street from Bicester to Aylesbury.

*O. G. S. Crawford, *Archaeology in the Field,* p.74

7 *Roman road across Blackstone Edge out of Lancashire into Yorkshire. Rough moor-stones are embedded in sand and rubble to a width of 16 ft and have a paved track, now worn to a channel, down the middle. This is probably the best preserved section of Roman road in Britain*

The roads that linked the administrative centres were made subject to Roman law in two divisions, public and private, with the distinction that the soil in the latter remained in private ownership and was public only for right of passage. These private roads developed into cross-country routes for commerce; the public roads tended to be defined in relation to parish and county boundaries, and were under the control of an Inspector-in-Chief. They continued to be national responsibilities until the Roman withdrawal, when they reverted to local control and became indistinguishable from private roads.

Stukeley was the first English antiquary to note carefully the construction of Roman roads. He recorded that he found part of Ermine Street north of Huntingdon paved, and the Fosse Way south of Ilchester 'composed of the flat quarry stones of the country, of good breadth, laid edgewise' so close that they looked 'like the side of a wall broken down'. He found similar stones for several miles near Willoughby-in-the-Wolds, Lincolnshire, at the other end of the Fosse, and heard it reported that this paving continued all the way from Newark to Leicester.* So again the Fosse Way derived great benefit from the stone

*Itinerarium Curiosum, p.155

along its course. In fact, when part of the Way south of Radstock was opened up in 1881 the full elaboration of Roman construction was recorded as being in five layers: (1) an earth foundation beaten to a hard surface; (2) large stones, some bedded in mortar; (3) small stones well mixed with mortar; (4) lime or chalk with powdered brick and tile; (5) sand and gravel.

But it must not be thought that all Roman roads conformed to this standard. In the early years of the Occupation the availability of material was inevitably the determining factor. Slag and cinders left over from iron-smelting were used in the South-East for roads across the Weald. The London to Brighton road had such a foundation in parts. In Essex and East Anglia this kind of material was not available, so construction might be of dried marsh-mud rammed hard between two rows of oak piles about four feet long, braced by timber cills. These mud beds would be packed with flints or rammed chalk, and surfaced with gravel. In other parts of the country marshes would be crossed by roads with brushwood foundations such as have already been described in the causeways of the Somerset Levels. In the North of England, where stone was plentiful, rough blocks of granite would be laid to form a track, which would be so strong that only a surfacing of gravel or stone chippings would be required to complete it. Even the final amenity of surfacing was dispensed with where the road was only required to bring metal from the mines into the towns, a tradition that ultimately gave rise to constructing the roads inside the Lancashire mill towns with cubes of millstone grit. So there was no common factor in the making of Roman roads beyond the basic one of a raised track, called an *agger,* with side ditches to carry off the rainwater.

The danger of drawing hasty conclusions from the straightness of old roads has already been mentioned; but even the degree of straightness that can properly be attributed to them may be an over-simplification. Nor need it necessarily be attributed to the Romans where it exists. Many of the prehistoric trackways that were not adopted by the Romans were straight. There is no mystery in such an alignment. Before ownership of land was established in law the shortest line between two given points was the obvious one to take if no obstacle such as a swamp or belt of trees obtruded, and directness could be achieved simply by smoke signalling from hilltops. In the South of England roads could be run for great distances along an approximately straight line without recourse to professional surveying or 'Old Straight Track' superstitions. The Romans adopted this existing logical basis for roadway alignment in Britain as they had done elsewhere; but with them straightness became a positive aim that must be followed even across marshes and in low-lying country where the existing roads were winding trails that had been rudely strengthened and embanked. They were able to do this because they could direct prisoners-of-war and local gangs commandeered from a conquered and submissive population to clear the woodlands through which the animals had established the existing trails, and to drain the marshes. Their modification was only allowed where hills were precipitously steep. In these circumstances slight detours might be introduced, but sooner or later the original line would be regained.

Crawford suggests that this clearing of woodland was the major benefit derived from the Roman occupation, and he may well be right. Unfortunately in southern England, where the soil is deep and Nature's resurgence vigorous, it is impossible to assess with

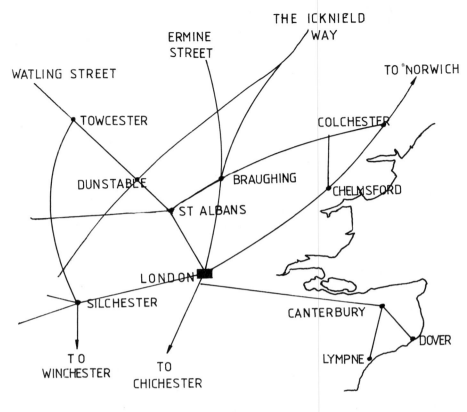

Map 3 Main Roman roads from London

anything approaching accuracy how much woodland was cleared. But in the North, where there are large areas in which woodland was not a factor, and where there was rock immediately below the surface the line of a Roman road may scarcely have been so much as modified. The road from Manchester to Preston survived in good shape until the coaching age simply because it had a foundation of natural rock for miles at a stretch, with little vegetation to encroach on it. There were many such roads in the North.

The six principal roads coming into London in Roman times were: (1) the road from Canterbury, with links from the Channel ports; (2) Stane Street, coming in at London bridge from Chichester and the Downs – a road that did not exist before the Romans made it; (3) the road from Silchester; (4) the road from Colchester, which was linked with the ancient Peddars Way that crossed Suffolk through Woolpit; and finally the two most important long-distance roads firmly established in Roman times: Watling Street coming in from the North-West and Ermine Street from the North-East of England.

Much confusion has arisen as a result of the extraordinary way in which these roads have changed their names. The road from Canterbury, now designated the southern part of Watling Street, has been the chief offender – or the one most offended against! According to Leland its earlier name had been Atheling (or Noble) Street. Certainly its

first appearance as Watling Street did not come until the beginning of the fourteenth century, by which time 'Watling Street' seems to have become a generic term for Roman roads, producing as many Watling Streets for roads as there are Avons for rivers. At one time part of it was known as the Milky Way, which begs another question, since there is a road in Scotland which is called both the Milky Way and Watling Street. Chaucer seems to have accepted both names for his pilgrims in the lines:

'now', quod he tho, 'cast up thyn ye;
See, yonder, lo, the Galaxye,
which men clapeth the Milky Way,
For hit is whyt: and some, parfey
Callen hit Watling Strete.'

Stow simply says that it was 'so named of the great highway of the same calling'. What matters now is that it followed the old Dover Road south of the Thames; but the present Watling Street should not be identified with it. As with Watling Street, there are several lengths of road called Ermine Street and Icknield Way that cannot be identified with the original. Some may have been branches of the main trunk, and like the branches of a tree have taken their names from the parent stem.

The true Watling Street was a highway of immense importance historically because it was the frontier established between the dominions of Alfred the Great and Guthrum, king of the Danes, by the Treaty of Wedmore. It left London by the Edgware Road to reach its first halting place at St Albans, then continued by way of Weedon in Northamptonshire to High Cross and Wroxeter. The A5 follows its route until it reaches the dog-leg south of Lichfield, where Watling Street ran over a peat bog. The odd thing is that although of such great historical importance and value for transport its course is not easily identified beyond Cannock Chase. The explanation is that like all our main roads it came under great strain when the Midlands were industrialised. Defoe said that in his day the northern part was only passable in the middle of summer when the 'coal carriages have beaten the way'. He alleges that after rain it became a ditch with horses sinking into it up to their bellies. From Wroxeter two branches ran out, one to Carlisle, the other to Newcastle.

Ermine Street left London by the Kingsland Road to run through Stoke Newington, Tottenham and Edmonton, where it left the present route to go through Theobalds Park towards Cheshunt and Broxbourne. Beyond Ware it continued along the line of the Old North Road, passing near the Roman camp at Braughing, and through Buntingford to Royston, where it crossed the Icknield Way. It continued to Colsterworth, then passed through Coldharbour (always an indication of a nearby Roman road) to Ancaster and on to Lincoln through Bayard's Leap in sections known locally by such interesting names as 'High Dyke', 'Old Street', and 'The London Ramper', which must be derived from rampart. Incidentally, there is another Icknield Street near Ancaster. It seems that in the matter of naming roads Defoe was a more reliable witness than he was in some other matters. He correctly dismisses several of these 'Roman roads' in the *Tour* as inventions of romantic antiquaries who took the legends of monkish chroniclers on trust.

8 Watling Street, running south-east from Hockliffe through Bedfordshire

9 Ermine Street at Londonthorpe, near Grantham, Lincolnshire

Ermine Street, with its successors the Old North Road and the Great North Road, is still to me the one great historic highway in which the whole history of an English through-way from prehistoric trackway to modern motorway can be read, linking as it does the capital of England with the capital of Scotland.

In the North of England the physical nature of the landscape has always determined the alignment of roads, with the Pennines dominating the system. Of the two great mountain roads one crossed Stainmore from Bowes to run through Brough to the ancient capital of Appleby, and thence through Carlisle into Scotland. Startforth, near Barnard Castle, was 'the ford of the Roman Street', and two milestones identified as Roman have been found near the summit of Stainmore at Spital. Protection for this great highway was covered by forts at Greta Bridge, Bowes, Brough, and Kirkby Thore. The other mountain road so far north was the one over Shap, linking Kendal with Penrith. Within a mile or so of the main street of Kendal is the site of a Roman fort, and at the other end, in the ancient royal manor of Penrith, is an elegant crescent, now called Bishop's Terrace, which appears to be aligned along a prehistoric ditch and rampart.

These long-distance roads had posting stations where horses could be changed and watered while their riders regaled themselves in what were the forerunners of our wayside inns. Milestones marked out their course as direction indicators; but it has to be borne in mind that although the Roman mile measured one thousand paces it varied in length. The explanation of this is that Roman surveyors measured distances horizontally. So where the roads cross flat country the distances shown on the milestones are approximately the same as ours, where they cross mountains the present measurements are appreciably longer. I don't know whether comparisons have been made on a national scale, but on comparing the distances along two lengths of road with which I personally happen to be familiar, the one from Ribchester in Lancashire to Ilkley in Yorkshire, and the one from Colchester to London, I found that the latter was the same today as in Roman times, the former, which crosses the Pennines, was only two-thirds of its present distance when measured in Roman miles.

The best Roman milestones were pillars bearing the distance to the next station on the route and the name of the emperor in whose reign the stone was erected. A typical example found on the Fosse Way two miles from Leicester in 1771, and another found in 1879 where four roads intersect in the centre of Lincoln are preserved in museums. Complete stones are rare; but pedestals with holes in the top indicating that a pillar has been removed from them are fairly common. They are sometimes known locally as 'golden pots'. But the best known Roman milestones are the rudely cut 'moor stones' found in mountainous country where stone was plentiful, and especially along the Roman Wall. At least ten have been identified along the road from Chester through Lancashire into Cumbria. When we think of the thousands there must have been we can only conclude that most of them have been broken up and used either for building walls or repairing roads. I know of one in a gate-post. In all, there are probably between 50 and 60 Roman milestones remaining.

An interesting feature of some Roman milestones is that they are cut in steps like our own mounting blocks or steps. The reason for this is that stirrups were unknown in Roman times, so levels were provided in milestones for riders to mount.

As many of our county towns started as Roman forts, many of our smaller roadside towns started as posting stations. If we glance along the line of a Roman road with this in mind we see that these towns tend to be spaced to allow one day's travel between them – which would vary between ten and fifteen miles at most. Larger villages often owed their origin to a local inn, which was a valuable source of revenue to its owner for the disposal of surplus produce from his estate. In Norman times these local inns were superseded in many places by the guest houses of abbeys; but with the Dissolution they returned to private ownership, and this, no doubt, explains the popularity of what is called 'Brewer's Tudor'.

The vehicles the Romans travelled in were obviously different from ours; but great advances were made on the primitive war chariots and transport waggons we used to see illustrated in school text books. When civilised life became organised a lightweight two-wheeled open carriage became popular. It was so sensible in design that it remained in use as long as the horse continued to be used for family transport, finally taking the form of the 'gig'. For the well-to-do there were the four-wheelers drawn by two horses, which also continued in use in improved form into the present century, while for ordinary citizens the wagonettes that some of us remember were anticipated by a Roman public conveyance. Finally came the lavishly ornamented four-wheeled carriages favoured by the nobility, which reached a luxurious standard. Some were actually made of solid silver, drawn by horses or mules with trappings embossed with gold. Gibbon tells us that Roman noblemen were in the habit of 'measuring their rank and consequence according to the loftiness of their chariots and the weight and magnificence of their dress', which all sounds very familiar, and shows how little human nature has changed in its more immature manifestations.

Taking an aerial view, as it were, of the Occupation, we may feel that the differences noted at the beginning of the period between the Belgic parts of the country and the British or Celtic were as great when the Romans left as when they landed. Cities had been built, each with its four principal streets running towards the four cardinal points of the compass from a central praetorium. With its forum, theatre, and public baths, each of these cities was a replica of the cities of Italy, based on Rome itself. In these, sedan chairs and litters became common, borne by tall handsome slaves who reflected the dignity of their masters. But in the hills of the North of England, the West, and the densely afforested parts of the Midlands the British lived on, still supporting themselves, as they were happy to do, by hunting, fishing and tending their flocks and herds. Even in the towns the bulk of the population never became Romanised.

So, while it was inevitable that much in the formal way of life that the Romans valued so highly disappeared with them, never to return, one thing they valued, their love of travel, has returned with a vengeance in the present century and accounts for the interest now being taken in the roads they made.

CHAPTER THREE

Anglo-Saxon and Scandinavian Farm-Ways and Market-Ways

THE ROADS trodden out by the Saxons were more like the cattle-trails of the Celts than the through-ways of the Romans. Lacking the wealth of Rome, and its authority to direct labour from the fields for road-making, the Saxons had to justify every length of new road by its value to their own local and largely self-contained communities. Long-distance travel seldom entered into the reckoning. Trade with the Continent practically dried up under them.

To understand this we need to bear in mind that generally speaking the Saxons were immigrants rather than invaders. Most of them came as pioneer farmers who had been crowded out of their homeland and were looking for nothing more ambitious than a plot of land to settle on and cultivate. In the South-East, where the land suited them best, there were no massive confrontations, and although their occupation became virtually complete, they did not massacre the natives. Ethnic research indicates considerable co-existence.

In the West of England they had to conquer before they could inhabit, and Bede bears witness to their prowess in this other 'field' in the Anglo-Saxon Chronicle, where we read how the Saxon forces under Cerdic defeated the British at Charford in AD519, and 'from that day on the princes of the West Saxons have reigned.' Alfred the Great's statue at Winchester is a permanent reminder of the Saxon conquest of Wessex.

The Saxon landings in the South-East extended over a period of more than 200 years. Cocking snooks, as it were, at the command of the Count of Saxon Shore, they rowed up the rivers in small boats under cover of darkness or when a mist lay over the marshes, to encamp between half-a-mile and a mile from the rich loam terraces of river banks. From these they worked their way inland, clearing scrub and draining swamps to provide pasture for their cattle and new land to cultivate. The pattern of these clearings is perpetuated in the many elongated parishes along the Thames Estuary and the Sussex coast, which frequently extend ten or more miles inland from a narrow riverside or coastal frontage.

Each of these early settlements would be established by a group of families, called *ingas,* or even by a single family, and the head of each gave his name to the village that more than 1,300 years later still bears it. From this custom we are able to identify places with names ending in -ing and -ham with personal prefixes as early Saxon settlements.

These were followed by the commoner Anglo-Saxon settlements which can be identified by names ending in -ton, and later by those with descriptive endings like -field, -stead, and -hurst, indicating the clearing of woodland. All were later to acquire secondary settlements, which can be identified by names ending in -tye and -end in Essex, -den in Kent, -fold in Sussex and so forth, with -green universal. All started as single farmsteads, and most of them have never become more than hamlets. At Domesday, for example, Wheathampstead in Hertfordshire, which then included Harpenden, had 19 -ends and 18 -greens.

These settlements were linked to each other by tracks that began as driftways for cattle and eventually developed into the spider's web of bridleways that are so characteristic of Saxon country. So everywhere in these highly cultivated counties we find today green lanes and blind lanes that appear to lead nowhere, and are so different from the better planned but less attractive byways of the Scandinavian Midlands and North. Along the Essex/Suffolk border they were the subject of such paintings as 'The Cornfield', suggesting that to Constable they were as characteristic of the countryside he loved as Dorset heaths were to Hardy or Lakeland fells to Wordsworth.

The villages served by these two distinct systems of byways may be divided into compact – sometimes called nucleated, or clustered – and scattered. Compact Saxon villages had a green in the centre, and were usually surrounded by open fields of arable land, whereas scattered villages were usually found in heavily wooded areas where clearing had been slow and erratic. We still find these old forest settlements, linked by winding lanes that thread their way through remnants of ancient woodland in the Chiltern beechwoods, where the timber gave rise to industries which supported a local way of life for centuries. The Chilterns are an excellent example of the slowness of woodland settlement, because before it became centred in High Wycombe, chair-making was carried on in small cottages grouped irregularly in forest clearings across the entire region.

In the mountainous North and West of England we find hill villages characteristic of sheep-rearing communities, each ringed with small walled enclosures, that may be called garths in one place and crofts in another, to contain the few cattle required traditionally to meet local needs. Most of the cottages have single apple trees; most of the farmhouses sheltering clumps of trees. These hillside settlements extend with only minor local variations from Cumbria and the Pennines to the Derbyshire Peak and from there into Shropshire and Wales. Many are still linked by gritty lanes with wide grass verges and drystone walls, along which countless herds of cattle and flocks of sheep were driven annually from Wales in the West and Scotland in the North.

William Page, a forerunner of W. G. Hoskins as an outstandingly perceptive student of the English landscape, analysed these typically English villages into four groups: (1) scattered; (2) clustered, off main roads; (3) clustered, on main roads; (4) ring-fence villages.* Early self-contained villages were usually off the highways. Like towns they were frequently sited at cross-roads or near fords, and these tended to become the more prosperous when the roads began to carry long-distance traffic. They then became street-

*'On the Types of English Villages and their Distribution' *Antiquity,* December 1927

villages, which in sheep-rearing country were almost invariably built with houses sufficiently far apart to accommodate street-markets with pens along both sides of the highway. This type is particularly characteristic of the Cotswolds, where one of the most familiar must be Moreton-in-Marsh, for which the lord of the manor obtained the grant of a market from Henry III.

In the East of England fear of invaders delayed the founding of roadside settlements until a strong central government had been established. This consideration was not a factor in the Cotswolds, where most of the main roads ran along the ridgeways and villages were established along the streams that ran through the valleys between them, adding so much to their charm today—as does the fact that the main roads still bypass them along the ridgeways.

The most interesting roads inside the villages are the back lanes, which began as driftways for cattle being driven into the fields and on to the outlying commons of the parish during the time when most of the farmhouses in lowland country were clustered together, not scattered as they are now. While walking along these back lanes we need to be on the look-out for names that provide clues to former uses, such as Mill Lane or Cattlegate. Most of these would be pastoral in implication; but names do occur that provide clues to vanished local industries or customs of which no other record remains. Names die hard.

The countryside along county boundaries is commonly found to be the most unspoilt and worthy of study by the landscape historian. This is certainly true of the Essex-Hertfordshire, the Essex-Suffolk, the Somerset-Devon, and many other border regions one could name. East Hertfordshire, which was formerly the fringe area of the East Saxon kingdom, is almost incredibly rural despite its proximity to London. The river Lea, which was an effective barrier to cross-country roads before the creation of the county of Hertford, clearly contributed to this, notwithstanding the prehistoric trackway along its banks and the importance of Waltham Abbey.

The two main contributory factors to the preservation of ancient features along county boundaries are: first, the obvious one that as they were the farthest removed from the administrative centre they tended to be neglected and, secondly, that they had the river that formed the county boundary flowing through them, which meant that they might be liable to flood in winter. This was certainly the case with the Essex-Hertfordshire border, which was so bedevilled by floods in rainy seasons that provisions had to be made for the North Road to leave London on two legs: one from Shoreditch through Ware, Royston and Huntingdon, the other from Holborn through Highgate, Stevenage and Biggleswade to Alconbury, where they converged. At least 15 English rivers form county boundaries, and all have permanently affected the development of the countryside along their banks between bridge towns. So while river banks were settled early by the Saxons, who made more use of river ways than of road ways for their original settlements, the Domesday villages found all along the banks have developed far less than the roadside settlements.

While still thinking of the Essex-Hertfordshire border, Ongar on the Essex side of the region might be noted for its similarity to Braughing on the Hertfordshire side, already mentioned in relation to Roman roads. Both are heads of Hundreds laced with fascinating webs of lanes linking isolated ancient parish churches. In fact, every stage of roadway development can be studied within these two parishes and their immediate vicinity. Above everything else they illustrate how local Saxon roads were, and in how many of them the centre has shifted.

There are particular local explanations for these movements; but the general explanation of why so many Saxon villages are off and not on the roads left by the Romans is that these were too valuable as quarries for the modest building requirements of the new settlers to be left intact, especially in counties like Essex, which lacked local stone. William Page probably made the distinction between 'on' and 'off' clustered villages because they are so often found to have different datings. Many roadside villages and small market towns have parent hamlets nearby, in which the mother church of the parish is found—often with Roman bricks in their walls.

But although the Saxons bypassed the main Roman roads in this way, they seldom bypassed ancient summerways. Most of the country they settled was liberally provided with these and with all that they made available for the basic needs of life. Such ancient trackways as the Icknield Way and the Peddars Way in East Anglia were also settled continuously – in both cases because they ran through countryside that had been heavily populated since prehistoric times.

In urban England the story was different. The Anglo-Saxons never dovetailed into the urban culture as they did into the kind of rural culture that had continued throughout the Occupation in South-East England. If it is objected that there is little evidence for this statement, the Saxon period being so inadequately documented, it can now be replied that aerial photography is rapidly increasing our knowledge of Saxon England, and showing that there was an agricultural way of life established in the South-East long before the arrival of the people we now associate with it. In fact, some of the field patterns may go back to Iron Age farmers and indicate continuous cultivation for more than 2,000 years. Such places as Hertingfordbury, now a suburb of Hertford, have certainly been occupied since the Iron Age.

Within this general picture there were local variations that had decisive effects on the cultivation of their respective roadway systems. Those of Kent and Sussex are remarkably different from those of Essex and Hertfordshire, and even from each other. The lanes of Essex twist and turn without rhyme – if not without reason – giving an aspect of defiant wildness to the far-flung scene. It may have been memories of his childhood on the edge of Epping Forest, as much as Inversnaid itself that prompted Gerard Manley Hopkins to write:

> *What would the world be, once bereft*
> *Of wet and of wildness? Let them be left,*
> *O let them be left, wildness and wet;*
> *Long live the weeds and the wilderness yet.*

In Kent and Sussex, by contrast, the farms give the impression of always having been more carefully planned, with clearly defined arable land near the farmstead and sheep or swine pastures at a distance, as we know they were from such names as Tenterden, which means the swine pasture of the people of Thanet. In Sussex the driftways between the farmsteads and their pastures are seldom circuitous as they are in Essex and in some parts of Kent, but tend to form a series of parallel tracks running up the slopes of the downs. In the Billinghurst district, where many tracks are roughly parallel with Stane Street,* they appear to date from the Romano-British period, and may be compared with lanes near Braughing, which are sprigs of Roman roads that converged there. But whilst these Romano-British associations are valid in both Sussex and Hertfordshire so long as we are in the valleys, on the uplands many of the tracks are clearly prehistoric and related to the barrows of the Bronze Age. From the earliest times these downland cattle-ways could be comparatively straight, and on the simple north-south alignment that makes them so different from the driftways of the Weald.

In neighbouring Hampshire, where cattle-breeding and sheep-grazing were to be developed on a larger scale, and where great fairs were held annually for the sale of cattle and sheep being driven in from Wales, the ancient trackways that converged on Salisbury Plain were kept open as drove roads converging on Andover, situated at the crossing of two Roman roads, a town that developed even in Saxon times into an important centre for wool from the sheep sold at Weyhill Fair.

The settlement of the Saxon kingdoms was so complete, and the system of cultivation so continuous that not until the present century was there any attempt to adapt their local roads for through traffic. In Sussex this would have been difficult because two geographical factors remained dominant: the Weald and the Downs. Now we have a series of motorways between London and the coastal resorts of Kent and Sussex super-imposed on this ancient landscape.

As Saxon roads were as localised as their names were personalised, the names they bear are peculiarly revealing. They were chosen with the sole object of clear identification. This was achieved with Watling Street and Ermine Street in the way we have seen. Most roads, however, were made identifiable by adding their purpose, locality, or specific character to the common base of *weg,* which means 'way'. As *port* meant market, portways were market ways. By the same token boundary ways were classified as *maer-wegs,* and these were to prove especially important and permanent because so many Saxon boundaries were adopted for parish boundaries. In Berkshire, and no doubt elsewhere, parish boundaries are still called 'meres', as are the boundary stones of Epping Forest.

Dr G. B. Grundy, who did such valuable work on Saxon charters, tells us that the words *maer* and *gemaere* were originally used specifically for balks – the uncultivated strips between ploughed furlongs. In course of time the tracks along these balks, first used to avoid damaging crops, became permanent roads, and this explains why so many right-angled bends are still found in roads that follow parish boundaries. Throughout most of our history, as we shall see later, the cost of maintaining roads was a local responsibility, and local authorities found them so important in defining boundaries for purposes of civil and ecclesiastical jurisdiction that any attempt to re-align them would have been supressed at once. However illogical the arguments for retaining their original lines might become, the clergy at all events could be relied upon to guard them

*Peter Brandon, *The Sussex Landscape,* Hodder and Stoughton, p.74

jealously while their tithes were at stake. So we had the annual ceremony of 'walking the bounds' of the parish, leaving us with such names as Paternoster Hill and Amen Corner, which marked a halt made to say the Lord's Prayer or repeat a pious invocation, and at the same time allow the elderly priest to recover his breath. From all this we may conclude that lanes and roads following parish boundaries are always ancient.

Most of these tracks remained unstrengthened until well into the Middle Ages. Such farm carts as there were would be either platforms or boxes – forerunners of the 'tub' – on roughly cut axles between a pair of wheels that might be as much as a foot wide, and were little more than logs cut from the trunk of a tree. The object in retaining this primitive form of transport for farm use was that the wide wheels acted as rollers for consolidating the turf. But in general, packhorses were more suitable for carrying produce to market. The number of terms associated with packhorses and pannier transport, some of which are given in the glossary at this end of this book, show how universal this form of transport must have been.

When we move north from the Home Counties or the West of England into the Midlands we cross country that was densely afforested in the Dark Ages, and eventually reach the stone belt which extends from Dorset to Northumberland, in which the lower fertility of the soil did as much to reduce the number of settlements as the forests of the Midlands ever did. The people occupying this region were of a different type from those of either the South or the West. It was not by accident that in course of time the Midlands and the North of England became so highly industrialised and urbanised. This was the land that had been overrun by the Vikings, who from their earliest forays came organised for invasion and conquest. Their marching armies brought the Roman roads back into use, which would not be difficult since only those crossing bogs would have deteriorated seriously. In the hills they had solid rock as their foundation, and any breaks could be repaired from nearby quarries.

This new landscape is harder and more positive. There are fewer green and blind lanes intercepting the long straight throughways that appear to take on personality and know precisely where they are going, and intend reaching it in the shortest possible time. Small emotive features that mean so much in the paintings of Constable become insignificant in so purposeful a landscape. The villages too are compact and orderly, with church and manor house close to each other.

We still call these 'the Shires', the name derived from the system of government imposed upon them by the Danes from such shire capitals as Lincoln, Nottingham, Leicester, and Derby. Contrary to popular belief, a shire is not a shearing but an administrative area.

From these shire capitals the rule of law was established and enforced in a way it never was before the Norman Conquest in Anglo-Saxon country, where custom alone determined practice – and rule by custom was not difficult in country where most of the inhabitants never left the parish in which they were born and died, except on occasional visits to the nearest market town, which would normally be within walking distance of their home. Authority in these Saxon villages reposed in their own thanes, whose privileges were merged in those of the lord of the manor after the Norman Conquest.

In the mountainous country of the North-West of England pockets of Celts survived, and as they followed the same pastoral pursuits as the invaders, integration was easy. In this kind of country, with its traditional way of life so firmly established there is little to be said about the roads. Geology determined their course. We do, however, get variations of the linear type of village, especially in the narrower dales of Derbyshire. The commonest of these is where short branches of the main street run up a steep slope, usually called a 'bank', a word that continues in use locally even when such precise names as 'nab' and 'scar' appear in official documentation.

In the larger Derbyshire villages these 'banks' lead to terraces running parallel with the main street below them. The explanation of this development is that water is available along the slopes from shallow wells that tap fissures in the limestone. As water is plentiful in the Peak, fully independent hillside hamlets, linked to each other by hard-surfaced, well-drained roads are found – which may now serve small mining and quarrying industries as well as stock-rearing.

Crossing from the North-West to the North-East of England we find in the old East Riding of Yorkshire a land settled by Angles, who made their first homes on the foothills of the Wolds, and from there spread across the Vale of York to Ripon and the Valley of the Ouse. Later they crossed the Pennines through the Aire Gap into Craven and the Ribble Valley, leaving traces of their colonisation in place-names with -ley endings, such as Otley and Ilkley in Wharfedale, Ripley, Pateley, and Darley in Nidderdale, and many -tons and -leys in Durham, running up Teesdale to the fells, where we get the -setts, -scales, and -gills of the Scandinavians. In Sleddale we even get the Scandinavian 'dale' added to the Old English 'slade', two words that have the same meaning. At the height of Anglian power their king, Ida, ruled from his castle at Bamburgh, a kingdom extending from the Tweed to the Humber.

The Danes filled in the land between these Anglian pockets and there is little to distinguish their respective settlements. The Danish can only be identified through the -by and -thorpe endings in village names. So the minor roads of the North-East are similar to those of all the eastern counties, with village greens at the heart of the villages they link, and traces of common fields on the outskirts. They have the straight lengths running along parish boundaries, with the double right-angled bends that we find as far south as Essex.

The Norman lay-out of so many villages in the North of England may surprise those who are not aware of the ruthlessness of William the Conqueror's punitive campaign of 1069 – the notorious 'harrying of the North' in which every church over a vast area was destroyed and every dwelling near it razed to the ground. It has been estimated that the devastation was so great in the East and North Ridings of Yorkshire that food production fell to one quarter of what it had been before the Conquest. Consequently, new villages on the Norman feudal plan were built by the Norman lords, with triangular greens or market-places dominated by a castle, often with a church near it. There is a concentration of such villages near Carlisle, and they are common throughout Cumberland, Westmorland, Durham, and Yorkshire.

When we reach Stainmore from Teesdale we climb into the Cumbrian landscape created by the sheep of the Norsemen, who settled these bleak fells in the first half of the tenth century from prehistoric trackways and Roman roads across Stainmore and Shap.

As the land above the forest belts round Penrith and Appleby, and extending eastwards into Lunedale, Balderdale, and Deepdale was almost entirely unoccupied when they landed in Morecambe Bay from Ireland, they were able to create small settlements on the pattern of those in their homeland in western Norway, and the period they had spent in Ireland since leaving Norway was commemorated in Norse-Irish place-names like Rey-cross, Staincross, and others incorporating 'cross' on Stainmore.

The Norse needed few local roads for such carts as they had, and it has been a remarkable characteristic of their descendants down to our own day, that they have continued to drive across the fells as their ancestors did, standing upright, with the reins held tightly in their hands as they swing themselves to and fro to balance the weight between the wheels when driving over rough ground.

CHAPTER FOUR

Medieval Roads, Bridges and Pilgrim Ways

———◆◆◆———

ALTHOUGH VILLAGES were rebuilt and the countryside reorganised after the Conquest, few long-distance roads of any consequence were made. Part of the reason for this is that many Roman roads were still capable of repair; but the main part of it is that once conquest had been accomplished the local roads of the Anglo-Saxons and Scandinavians, which by this time practically covered the country, were adequate for a parochial system of government that could readily be adapted to a manorial system of control.

In the South of England the basic elements of feudalism were so firmly established in the local administration of the thanes, that all that was needed was for their status to be reduced to that of five-hide farmers, made subject to Norman barons seated in their castles at the heart of large estates called 'honours'. There were a thousand such castles by the middle of the twelfth century, and countless religious houses occupied by French monks. The barons and the abbots between them had the future in their hands, and they took full advantage of their power until the final step was reached by replacing the Saxon kingdoms by counties administered from county towns.

In the North both Church and Castle were strong, with the Church outlasting the Castle in the exercise of power, especially by the Cistercians, who established themselves at Rievaulx in 1131 and at Fountains in 1132. Their abbots became the first great estate managers in our history, introducing new skills in animal-breeding, the effect of which is still not exhausted. Eventually the whole of the North of England became one vast sheep run,* bringing wealth from the wool to the abbeys as in other parts of England; but whereas in the South we have evidence of this wealth in great tithe-barns, so many of which are now in decay, in the North the harshness of the climate and the thinness of the soil kept life austere and frugal. The South also had a better start. At the Conquest even the Archbishopric of York was so poor that for two periods it was held in plurality with the wealthy See of Worcester.

In the East of England, Peterborough, Ely, and Bury St Edmunds became rich Benedictine abbeys, and across the counties that had been settled by the Danes the shire capitals became thriving urban communities, laying the foundations of the nation's provincial wealth under local overlords who were in the same kind of competition with

*A. M. Cooke, 'The Settlement of the Cistercians in England', *Eng. Hist. Rev.* (1893), p.625

the abbots as the manufacturers of the nineteenth century were to be with the landed gentry. Thus the abbots of the Middle Ages played a far greater part than the barons in remoulding the landscape, modified in the North by sporting interests in which both clerics and nobles shared. A glance at any touring map will show how extensively Cumbria was subject to the Forest Laws. Copeland Forest covered the western fells between the Derwent and the Esk. The greater part of Wordsworth's Duddon flowed through the Forest of Millom, which continued under the lordship of its owner until the estate was broken up in the eighteenth century. On the east, the forests of Grisedale, Thornthwaite, Fawcett and Sleddale all belonged to the barony of Westmorland, and as we drive through these dales today we can still see the scree-scarred ridges, with lynchets scraped out for crops by prehistoric farmers.

It is in such features as these that we are still able to read the evolution of the Lake District landscape, and not least of its road system, as a continuous narrative. Nowhere can this be seen better than from Crosthwaite, the mother church of Keswick, which dates from about 1175 and marks the site of the British settlement from which the region developed along tracks that still radiate from it through the Lakeland passes. Kendal has always been a more important hub of mountain routes than Keswick, but because these have become trunk roads their early character has become less apparent. Nor are survivals from ancient trackways confined to the mountains. At Cockerham, which is situated on the edge of the marsh drained by the river Cocker, a Premonstratensian abbey was built, sustained by the salt produced from the salt pans in the marshes. The abbey has gone but the saltways remain, all except one of them leading to Lancaster. The exception is now incorporated in the M6 motorway, which bypasses Lancaster on its way north to Penrith over Shap, where another Premonstratensian abbey was established. It is exciting to think that this road must have been used by the Norse shepherds who landed in Morecambe Bay between 899 and 915, leaving evidence of their point of arrival – or one of them – in the hogback tombstone at Heysham, now preserved inside the Church.

In both Lancashire and Yorkshire, where there was scope for a new road system to be developed, conditions remained stagnant until the abbots gained their full power, because in those counties as in Westmorland and Cumberland large areas were designated 'Royal Forest' and sterilised from progress. These extended over so much of Lancashire that as late as the eighteenth century William Cobbett noted that between Oldham and Newcastle, outside the towns, he did not see in a distance of 150 miles as many churches as would be seen in any 20 miles in the valleys of Wiltshire. And it was not only in the North that the clearing of woodland was curtailed in the interests of sport and excluded from the common law. Practically the whole of the Midland region now included in the geographical counties of Herefordshire, Worcestershire, Shropshire, and Cheshire was designated 'Royal Forest'; but the effect of that designation fluctuated from reign to reign. At one time the total area of the Royal Forests may have amounted to one-third of the kingdom; but even then the degree to which land could be cultivated varied according to the popularity of the region for sport. Where whole counties were included, as were Cornwall, Devon, Essex, Rutland, Leicestershire, Northamptonshire, and Lancashire, as well as the other counties named above, it would have been impossible to impose full restraints over the entire region. This was recognised by large sections of these counties being disafforested in the legal sense of the term in 1204, and the counties of Sussex, Lincolnshire, Leicestershire, and Middlesex obtaining full exemption in the same century.

As we find so often, the incidence of late Saxon and Scandinavian place-names is the best evidence we have of the progress of settlement in areas that were originally included in the Royal Forests, and the local roadway systems can often be interpreted from them. In Epping Forest, for example, which continued to be popular with royal hunters and their favourites until late in the seventeenth century, we are still able to see how many of the minor roads now metalled must have begun as pilgrim trails to the Holy Cross at Waltham, and were later to be used by the Augustinian canons of Waltham who came out to serve their various chapels of ease when these were built in forest clearings. I have dealt with this briefly in my *Portrait of Epping Forest* (1977), but the subject can be dealt with much more comprehensively in relation to the New Forest, where the chroniclers of the twelfth century lamented that the Conqueror had reduced a flourishing cultivated area to a waste, destroying whole villages and demolishing churches. It is now thought that this can have applied only to the fringe of the Forest, most of which must have been waste when William designated it forest. But by extending the area and arresting development he did segregate it and we are now able to study ancient trackways that have never had a later culture superimposed on them*.

Of the counties of mixed cultivation, probably the best in which to study continuity of use of the same routes over long periods is Devon. On Dartmoor, as in the Lake District, the tracks used by the monks and preaching friars were first made by prehistoric farmers who enclosed their cattle in small crofts and drove them on to the moors for pasture. As we shall see later, when coach roads were made they bypassed the lanes formed to serve the -hayes and -worths, which explains why the deep lanes of Devon continue as hollow ways with a vengeance, their tortuous routes indicating the early cultivation of scraps of moorland laboriously ploughed and banked off. Personally, I have often wondered how many of them were built at such immense labour in order to keep the deer off the cultivated enclosures. Those who know how necessary it is to have both a ditch and either high banks or hedgerows along both sides of it if the roam of deer is to be effectively restricted, might agree that the idea is not wholly fanciful.

In the Lake District the wall to Nab Scar from Rydal Water was built for the contrary purpose of preventing Grasmere cattle straying into the deer forest of Rydal. It would certainly not have prevented the deer straying in the opposite direction. A more comparable barrier in the Lake District was the dyke of earth stabilised with stones, parts of which survive, of an enclosure made in 1290 when the monks of Furness were given permission to enclose about 30 acres of pasture near Buttericket in Eskdale with a 'dyke, wall, or palings'; but in this case it had to be one that the deer in the adjoining Forest of Egremont could leap.

The respective influences of Church and Castle are frequently shown in the names of roads. Devon has its Abbot's Way, which ran from Buckfastleigh to Buckland, with a

*F. H. Baring, 'The Making of the New Forest', *Eng. Hist. Rev.* (1901)

branch to Tavistock, while its alternative name of Jobbers' Lane reflects the wool interests of the Church, since the jobbers in question must have been yarn-jobbers. Sometimes the interests of Church and Castle were combined, as in more than one Earls-way. One in the North Midlands that was first recorded in 1200 was clearly constructed by the earls of Chester for their own convenience in visiting outlying estates and that of their tenants in visiting markets. It linked Chester with Nottingham, Leicester, Derby, and Leek, and survives in such local names as Yelsway, near Waterhouses in Notting-hamshire. But another road constructed by the earls of Chester, which ran from Leek to Macclesfield, was to enable the monks who had been moved from a place near the Welsh border to a secluded valley near Leek to collect wool from the abbot's granges and carry it for export to Chester.

At the height of their prosperity the princes of the Church had unrivalled power and travelled as befitted such potentates. The Bishop of Durham had a private army at his command, and saw to it that he had roads along which his troops could reach the Border. The Bishop of Winchester, with palaces widely dispersed across Hampshire, travelled like a Sovereign on his episcopal visitations. One of the greatest 'princes', William of Wykeham, Chancellor of England as well as Bishop of Winchester, repaired many roads within the diocese as well as the highway and all the bridges along its course between his palaces at Winchester and Southwark. Not all accounts of episcopal pomp have sur-vived; but we know that Richard de Swinfield, Bishop of Hereford, moved from one of his manors to another attended by squires, clerks of the chapel, kitchen servants, bakers and so forth, including a 'champion', who turns out to have been a lawyer retained to defend the bishop's interests in any lawsuit incurred on these travels. Some bishops even took their falconers with them.

Markets and Fairs

The best guide to the economic progress of the common people during the Middle Ages is the record of the granting of markets, which could only be established by charter, and were strictly regulated. So many were granted during the thirteenth century that in 1256 Henry de Bracton, or Bretton, produced a treatise setting out the principles which he, as a judge of wide experience, considered should determine the question of any grant. The basic principle was that they should not be nearer each other than would be required for a man to travel both ways and do his business by daylight. The effect of this principle is that to this day there are few places in England away from mountain ranges that are not within seven miles of a market town. The reason for this spacing being adopted is that if the day were divided into three equal parts both as regards time and the expenditure of energy, this would fill the daylight hours even in winter, and in summer would allow time for diversion; but in limiting in this way the distance that local people would have to travel in going about their lawful occasions it is not unduly cynical to feel that the owners had their own interests in mind when concurring.

It was quickly recognised that the prosperity of a market depended on the roads leading up to it. Most of these were already there; but many were no more than green lanes with hedgerows behind which robbers could lurk. Under Anglo-Saxon law a traveller had been required to give warning of his approach by sounding a horn: 'If a far-coming man, or a stranger, journey through a wood, and neither shout nor blow his horn, he is to be held for a thief and either slain or redeemed.'

With the establishment of markets, safety for those attending them became the all-important factor. So it became normal to insert clauses in grants providing for the safe-conduct of merchants. The local people would often travel together for mutual protection. We have a constant reminder of this concern for safety in the words of the Litany: 'That it may please Thee to preserve all that travel by land or by water, all women labouring of child, all sick persons, and young children; and to show Thy pity upon all prisoners and captives'.

In more practical terms this concern was taken care of in the Statute of Winchester (1285), which laid down that highways connecting market towns should be widened so that there was no ditch, tree, or bush in which a man might lurk to do mischief within 200 feet of either side of the road, with the mitigation that such trees as oaks and great beeches were excluded from the prohibition if the ground below their branches was clear. The responsibility for ensuring that these conditions were observed was placed on the shoulders of the lords of the manors through which the roads passed, and if robbery or murder ensued from neglect they were answerable at law and might have heavy penalties imposed upon them. This liability remained even if the land bordering the highway had been imparked.

Before this Act was passed it was already accepted that roads under the king's protection should be wide enough for two ox-waggons to pass on them, for two oxherds to make their goads touch across them, and for 16 armed knights to ride side by side along them.* It had been universally accepted before the Romans came that the four highways of Watling Street, Ermine Street, the Fosse and Icknield Ways enjoyed royal protection. During the Middle Ages this protection was extended to all the more important roads linking major boroughs and market towns—hence the term, the king's highway. The Sovereigns and greater nobles of the twelfth and thirteenth centuries reintroduced long-distance travel to an extent that had not existed since Roman times. This was especially so between England and France, from which the alien aristocracy, both lay and clerical, had come.

In the clay-lands of south-eastern England hundreds of miles of the grass verges of these medieval highways remain unenclosed, although many are now overgrown with the shrubs and brambles which the law forbade. They remind us that for centuries farm waggons would make their unsteady progress along them drawn by oxen, retained until the eighteenth century in Essex and Sussex because their cloven hooves gave them better footing than horses had. These heavy waggons cut so deep into the soft clay during rainy seasons that several parallel tracks had to be brought into use, which meant that the wide roads introduced for public safety when most men travelled to market on horseback had to be retained when vehicular transport came into common use. And the restriction to the enclosing of grass verges was not maintained only for side roads liable to flood. The Hog's Back in Surrey is the best example of an ancient highway that has retained

*F. M. Stenton, *The Econ. Hist. Rev (1936) No. 1*

wide verges between ancient hedgerows although well drained and with excellent visibility all along its course.

As the price of wool, the foundation of the nation's prosperity throughout the Middle Ages, tended to rise and the profits from agriculture to fall, a new class of industrialist came into the wool towns, and gained respect by the liberal endowment of churches that were falling into decay, with the result that at the end of the fourteenth century there were many unclaimed and uncultivated strips in villages that had relied on open-field farming for a thousand years or more, and where the local road system had never developed beyond what was required to meet the needs of self-contained communities. This resulted in the early enclosure of Kent, Essex and East Anglia in the East, and Devon and Cornwall in the West.

With the growth of long-distance travel came the growth of the great fairs, from which towns might even take their shape. At St Ives in Huntingdonshire, where one of the four great fairs of England was held, Bridge Street was the main thoroughfare, with minor streets branching off it along which rows of stalls and booths of visiting skinners, butchers, and ironmongers were set up. Tracks on St Giles's Hill, Winchester, are clearly fairground tracks. Greatest of all the fairs was Stourbridge, the prototype of Bunyan's 'Vanity Fair', which is described by Thorold Rogers as the place to which 'the Venetian and Genoese merchant came with his precious stock of Eastern produce, his Italian silks and velvets, his store of delicate glass; the Flemish weaver was present with his linen of Liège and Ghent' and so forth. All this valuable merchandise had to be brought to the fair by road from the ports of Lynn and Blakeney, while trains of packhorses brought tin from Cornwall, lead from Derbyshire, and iron ore from the forges of the Forest of Dean or from Sussex. The marvel is that even the through-roads could cope with such traffic after their long period of neglect. Certainly the maintenance of the Icknield Way and Ermine Street became vital. That is why in 1252 we find Henry III ordering the sheriff to clear part of what is now the Great North Road of underwood against ambushes.

During the twelfth and thirteenth centuries practically all the great historic fairs became chartered and were reconstituted to conform with the prosperous fairs of the Continent, thus in a sense anticipating the Common Market of the twentieth century. Troy weight takes its name from Troyes Fair in France, and much of our banking system originated in the system devised for the fairs of Champagne.

After the dissolution of the monasteries the town markets were further developed by such families as the Howards, Nevilles, Percies, and Stanleys. A market franchise had become a valuable asset. With their development regular trade superseded annual or biannual fairs as the mainstay of local life, and farm carts and waggons came into general use.

Bridges

While most transport was by packhorses with panniers strapped to their saddles, fords served for crossing rivers except in times of flood. Bridges had been built by the Romans, but most of them were falling into decay by the time of the Norman Conquest. As the

need for them increased with the establishment of markets, most of which were originally for the benefit of the Church, it came about that the main contribution of the people
of the Middle Ages to the improvement of communications was in the building of
bridges, hundreds of which remain and should be given high priority for protection. The
bridge-building movement began before the end of the eleventh century and continued
unbroken until the abbeys were dissolved in the sixteenth. Guilds contributed generously
in the cities, mindful of the benefit to be derived from them. Bristol, in particular,
benefited from this source. So did Birmingham from the generosity of the Guild of the
Holy Cross, with an eye on the trade to be drawn from the Welsh Marches. The bridge
over the Thames at Abingdon was kept in repair by the Fraternity of the Holy Cross.

The question of who was responsible for the maintenance of the unendowed bridges
was long bedevilled by the fact that boundaries frequently ran down the middle of the
streams they spanned. There can be few if any counties in which records are not available
at county Record Offices of long drawn-out disputes between neighbouring authorities
as to which was responsible for the repair of a bridge, and when it came to rebuilding the
bridge one half might be done as much as a hundred years before the other. In fact, when
a new bridge was planned the project often took an intolerable length of time to get off
the ground because it was held that the Common Law of England required that whoever
built a bridge was responsible for its maintenance, which partly explains why legal
advisers to local authorities are still addicted to the phrase 'provided there is no

10 Medieval bridge over the Stour at Sturminster Newton, Dorset

commitment to any ongoing liability'. Furthermore, *Magna Carta* declared that 'No village or individual shall be compelled to make bridges at river banks except those who from of old were legally bound to do so'. This led to a mistaken belief that if 'those who from of old were legally bound to do so' could not be traced, no-one need worry.

In this climate of public opinion it was inevitable that the cost of repair rose to a figure far greater than a sparsely populated parish could reasonably be expected to bear. Fortunately, two remedies were introduced which between them proved singularly effective right through to the time when the keeping of bridges in good repair became the responsibility of the county in which they stood. One was the granting of 'pontage', or the right to collect tolls, which was the gift of the Crown to those who undertook to make themselves responsible for maintenance, and explains such curious names as 'Halfpenny Bridge'. No doubt many bridge-head towns on county boundaries straddle the river for the purpose of protecting the bridge and collecting tolls. There may, of course, have been other reasons, such as the manorial reason, which led to part of Woolwich being on the north bank of the Thames, although in that case at a point no bridge could straddle. Incidentally, in view of the number of bridges spanning the Thames today it is remarkable that there was not one between London Bridge in the City and Kingston until the eighteenth century.

The other solution was devised by that most resourceful of all fund-raisers, the Church. This was the system of getting the bridges repaired by designating their building and upkeep 'pious and meritorious works before God', and granting 'indulgences'—that is to say, remissions of punishments after sacramental absolution. This proved to be by far the most effective method. The best known instance of this is the early fourteenth century decree by Richard de Kellawe, Bishop of Durham, who 'persuaded that the minds of the faithful are more ready to attach themselves to pious works when they have received the salutary encouragement of fuller indulgencies, trusting in the mercy of God Almighty remitted 40 days of the penances imposed on all who were sincerely contrite and confessed of their sins, who shall help by their charitable gifts or by their bodily labour, in the building or in the maintenance of the causeway between Brotherton and Ferrybridge, where a great many people pass by'. John Fordham, Bishop of Ely, granted similar indulgences to the godly who worked on the repair of the road from Trumpington to Cambridge.

As early as the twelfth century an Order of Bridge Friars was constituted with special responsibility for bridges, and we have reminders of this pious aspect of bridge maintenance in the chapels preserved on the bridges at Wakefield, Bradford-on-Avon, Rotherham, and St Ives, in which masses were said for the souls of their benefactors. Nevertheless, curious doubts arose about the maintenance of some important causeways that should have been adequately documented. At Waltham Abbey in the Lea Valley the road from the Eleanor Cross to the abbey crossed a marsh along causeways with bridges, four of which were the responsibility of the abbot of Waltham; but apparently not all. When in 1294 Edward I ordered an enquiry into this, the jurors were unable to agree on either who built them or who was responsible for their repair, but found that two chaplains dwelling on the causeway repaired them out of alms. In short, they had found for themselves a good pitch!

11 Stopham Bridge over the River Rother, West Sussex: built 1309, repaired in the sixteenth and nineteenth centuries

The most famous causeway is that between Chippenham and Bremhill, built by Maud Heath, a pedlar woman who had to carry her country produce to market along this road, which in winter was frequently flooded by the Avon. At her death in 1474 she was found to have left land and houses to provide an income for the construction and maintenance of a causeway from Wick Hill to Chippenham. This is now a raised path about five miles long, which at its lowest point crosses the river on arches. In 1838 a life-size representation of Maud Heath was erected as a memorial to her. She is shown seated, grasping an oaken staff, with a basket laden with country produce beside her.

Leland was the first antiquary to leave notes on bridges, recording carefully which were of wood and which of stone. We are greatly indebted to him even if his dating is not reliable. He was clearly impressed by several in the North of England, where the rivers run deep, but where stone was at hand for bridges that would span them. Twizel Bridge, so called from the Old English word *twisla,* which means 'fork by a river', he described as 'of stone one bow, but great and stronge'. Other fine bridges in the North are at Haydon, built at the only point where the road into Scotland via Carlisle crosses the Tyne; Corbridge, with a thirteenth century bridge; Morpeth, where the piers of the medieval bridge can be seen alongside the one that succeeded it, and Durham's two noble bridges. Most of these northern bridges were built for martial rather than pious uses, as we know from the many that had defence towers where arms were stored, instead of chapels where masses were said. One survives at Warkworth, Northumberland. Those at Chester, York, and Durham have been removed.

Dorset is the outstanding county for medieval bridges in the South of England. At Wool, near the home of the Turberville, or D'Urberville, family is one remarkable for the massive proportions of its cut-waters, with recesses for foot-passengers. A 1343 record tells us that at that date it was and always had been 'maintained and repaired by alms', and nobody was under any obligation to repair it—an instance of the legal ambiguity already mentioned. Sturminster Marshall has a medieval bridge of eight arches with parapets corbelled out from the main structure, and this is surely the most beautiful bridge in Dorset. In 1341 it was known as the White Mill Bridge. Sturminster Newton also has a fine medieval bridge, widened by building over the cut-waters in the manner seen at Fordingbridge.

The oldest stone bridges have simple semi-circular arches. Pointed arches came in the fourteenth century and continued in the fifteenth, to be followed in the sixteenth by the four-centred Tudor arches which remained in favour until the second half of the seven-

12 The Town Bridge, Bradford-on-Avon, with pilgrims' chapel, used as a lock-up in the seventeenth century

teenth century. What is called the segmented arch, the name given to an arch that is only part of a semi-circle, remained popular throughout the entire period for simple bridges across minor streams or along the parts of causeways that were liable to flood. Crawford Bridge across the Tarrant, mentioned in the Charter of the abbey of Tarent in 1235, has segmented arches. Indulgences for its repair were granted in 1506. But most southern counties have these segmented arches, particularly in marshland.

When a new bridge was required to replace an existing one it was unusual for the original structure to be destroyed entirely. If the road was being realigned, as with the bridge over the Hodder at Mitton in the West Riding of Yorkshire (now in Lancashire), the old bridge was left to gather to itself local legends like moss. If the new bridge was required in the same position as the old one, the usual practice was to give the old bridge a new casing. An interesting example is the bridge over the Teign on the Teignmouth road at Newton Abbot in Devon. When this was being rebuilt in 1815 it was found that at least four strengthenings, or enlargings, were incorporated in the surviving structure. The earliest seemed to be Roman, which had been given a timber frame by the Normans, followed by two casings in stone in the thirteenth and sixteenth centuries.

With the decay of monasticism the bridges that had relied for their repair on 'pious and meritorious works before God' again fell into dilapidation, and many remained broken until in 1531 the Tudor Statute of Bridges empowered the Justices of the Peace to raise funds for their repair. At the Dissolution, which was completed within ten years of the passing of the Act, Henry VIII gave a lead in conveying lands from the dissolved Christ Church to Canterbury Cathedral 'in order that charity to the poor, the reparation of roads and bridges, and other pious offices of all kinds should multiply and spread afar'. His lead was not followed. It was hardly to be expected that it would be.

Pilgrim Ways

Another source of revenue that disappeared with the Tudor secularisation of society was the medieval veneration of relics, a superstition that had sustained an elaborate system of pilgrim routes for centuries in response to such appeals as that made in 1458 by the Bishop of Ely beginning: 'Since our church at Ely is surrounded by waters and marshes, and the relics of the Holy Virgin lying in it can only be visited over bridges and causeys, requiring daily repair, we commend to your charity William Grene, hermit, who at our command and with the consent of our church at Ely, has undertaken the repair of the causeys and bridges ...', and so forth.

Although this urge to go on pilgrimages had existed from time immemorial, as we know from the way Stonehenge had anticipated Canterbury, there is a date for the inception of Pilgrim Ways in the Christian Church as definite as that for the opening of a new stretch of motorway. They were instituted in 787 with the forbidding by the Seventh Council of Nicaea, under pain of excommunication, of the consecration of any church without a holy relic. This resulted in such a scramble for relics or what could be passed off as such that at the height of the fever there were no fewer than ten 'heads of John the Baptist'. Yet despite the multiplication of identical relics the faith of the pious remained undiminished until the fever either burnt itself out or found a new outlet. The

Map 4 Pilgrim shrines

outstanding example of the power to be derived from the possession of a shrine is Durham, where devotion to St Cuthbert led eventually to the bishops becoming princes palatine.

Most of the pilgrimages were sparked off by alleged miracles. Within 24 hours of the murder of Thomas à Becket at Canterbury a miracle was reported as far away as Berkshire, and it was the need to provide lodging for pilgrims that led to the establishment of hospices managed by lay brothers. Many of these were later to become inns, of which the best known are the 'George' at Glastonbury, the Hostel of the God-Begot at Winchester, the 'Falstaff' at Canterbury, the 'New Inn' at Gloucester, and the Pilgrims' Hostel at Battle. Several carry 'The Angel' as their sign. Such hostels must have determined the course of many present-day highways, since between the ones just named there must have been others along the routes to them. At every stage in the history of highways we find what has already been pointed out, and will continue to be repeated, that once long-distance routes have been established they have remarkable powers of survival. This was understandable before roads were shown on maps and travellers had to rely on personal knowledge; but I remember that when some of us were trying to persuade the Government of the day to provide hostels for ex-prisoners, with whom homelessness was a major problem in rehabilitation, it was found that the only ones that had any chance of being used were those in towns situated on the old 'tramp routes'.

The first of the English shrines to attract throngs of pilgrims was Glastonbury, and it could not have been more inconveniently situated. It was surrounded by swamps and reedy marshes across which herdsmen led their flocks during dry seasons only, as they had led them in the East in Old Testament times. On the other hand, no better site could have been found for the creation of the myth of Joseph of Arimathaea and the miraculous thorn than among the lake villages of Avalon that were to become the setting for the Arthurian romances. As most people now know, there is no foundation in fact for either Joseph's visit or the miraculous thorn. They were the invention of Irish monks for the purpose of raising money to rebuild the monastery founded by Ine at the beginning of the eighth century after it had been destroyed by fire in 1184. But the blarney was so successful that even Sir William Dugdale in the seventeenth century seems to have accepted it without question, piously recording that 'about sixty-three years after the Incarnation of Our Lord' Joseph of Arimathaea 'erected, to the honour of the Virgin Mary, of wreathed twigs, the first Christian Oratory in England'.

The time was opportune. The two ancient universities had been founded and were being visited by scholars from distance places. The Benedictines were even formulating plans for a system of political representation, and the atmosphere was being created for the building of the great cathedrals, which could not have been envisaged in a civilisation constituted in small groups of villages round market towns, with no more than a minster, or mother church, at the heart of each.

Glastonbury was by no means the only place of pilgrimage to be sited on an island in a desolate marsh, and the very isolation of such places may well have been seen as an advantage by those who founded them as being conducive to the monastic way of life. But as travel across marshland was hazardous, posts had to be erected to guide pilgrims. These were usually stones, like those on the pilgrim ways that ran from Chester and

Shrewsbury to the shrine of St Winifrede at Holywell on the Dee estuary. As most of these stones were uncarved they are sometimes attributed to the Romans. The origins of mark-stones has its own mythology. Fortunately Glastonbury had no need of them. Its signpost was the 500-foot tor.

After Glastonbury came Winchester, where the body of St Swithin had been buried in a humble grave on the north side of the cathedral. Obviously this would never impress pilgrims. So in 971 the body was exhumed and reburied in a shrine behind the high altar, where it attracted more pilgrims than any other shrine in England until Thomas à Becket's took the lead 200 years later. As Winchester was already well served with roads its success was assured.

The distance between Winchester and Canterbury was 120 miles. Some of this Pilgrims' Way is now lost; but approximately two-thirds of it is still traceable, with lengths of as much as 15 miles without a break, and its pilgrim use explains why several churches along it are dedicated to either St Swithin or St Thomas, some of which, how-ever, have had their dedications changed. The Hospital of St Cross at Winchester also continues to remind modern pilgrims to other 'shrines' that at this 'hospice for thirteen poor men' pilgrims could obtain a 'dole of bread and ale'.

Map 5 The Pilgrims' Way

We should be grateful that both Winchester, the capital of Wessex since 519, and Canterbury, the most cultivated city in south-east England, acquired shrines that did not require the importation of miracle-working relics to draw pilgrims to them, because this was the age in which a miracle-working relic could shift the local centre of power as surely as in our day the discovery of a seam of precious metal or a new oil-field can. But although the ancient link between these two capital cities remained, their relative wealth changed rapidly after the murder of Thomas à Becket. Within a few years of this event Winchester had lost most of its ancient fame and its connection with 'The Pilgrims' Way' as we now know it has to be seen in the context of these respectively changing fortunes.

This is not the place to take up the arguments over the disputed alternative routes which the original 'Pilgrims' Way' followed; but since the first reference to it by that name did not occur until 200 years after the Dissolution its historical importance may be thought to be less than that of many less publicised routes. What is to be noted in relation to the evolution of roadways is that for so much of its length it follows summerways, or terraces along the Downs, rather than the crest of the ridges, and that in some places it even becomes a hollow way, although obviously there would be no alternative to following the ridgeway of the Hog's Back, from which the old Pilgrims' Way ran in a straight line between the 200- and 300-foot contours on the northern slopes of Box Hill, and continued on high ground north of Reigate.

In East Anglia the route followed when the body of St Edmund was carried from St Edmundsbury to London for safety is less studied than it might be; but the Saxon church at Greensted, near Ongar, the only surviving timber-naved Saxon church in England, is a cherished shrine. It was here that the body of the saint rested on its return journey into Suffolk, and the authentic route, like that of the Pilgrims' Way south of the Thames is marked by ancient churches, many of which have now been bypassed by modern roads. As all these pilgrim ways had their parasites, or hangers-on—beggars, pardoners, sellers of trinkets and chapmen of various kinds, who would have taken shelter in the churches until the clatter of hooves or the singing of hymns signalled the approach of pilgrims—they must have had their hazards as well as their rewards. We know that palmers, who began as pilgrims able to claim that they had visited the Holy Land, were thought of in Chaucer's time as mountebanks, who worked their passage and got their living out of hypocritically assumed piety. No doubt this gave rise to the saying: 'You will have to grease his palm'. Langland describes such a palmer in the lines:

> *He bare him a staff with a broad strip bound,*
> *That round it was twined like a woodbine's twist;*
> *A bowl and a bag he bare by his side;*
> *A hundred of vials was set on his hat,*
> *Signs from Sinai, Gallician shells;*
> *With crosses on his cloak, and the keys of Rome,*
> *And the vernicle before, that men should discern*
> *And see by his signs what shrines he had sought.*

Among the tawdry ornaments sold at shrines, which took their name from St Audrey (St Etheldreda, patron saint of Ely), were tiny bells to be hung on the harness of the horses to cheer pilgrims along tedious stretches of the road, and at the same time to inform other wayfarers of the shrines already visited, much as motorists now acquire stickers that broadcast that they have seen the lions at Longleat or whatever the latest novelty may be. Canterbury bells, incidentally, take their name from these medieval baubles. Palmers obviously served a similar purpose for the Church in advertising shrines. Whether it was a self-defeating one in the end is for others to speculate upon. At all events Chaucer's Canterbury pilgrims were making their journey towards the end of the period and reflect its decline rather than its heyday. More permanent reminders of the association of roads with pilgrims and their hangers-on are the many Palmers' Ways, like

the one across Breckland from Brandon to Walsingham, and such delightful reminders of Chaucerian aspects of travel as 'Jugglers' Way', found east of Calne in Wiltshire.

Regrettably it has to be recorded that relics had to be guarded against covetous clerics as well as unprincipled laymen. Bede's bones were stolen from Jarrow by the sacrist in the eleventh century, and the story is told of Bishop Hugh of Lincoln, who was later canonised, that in 1199, while visiting the monastery of Fécamp, where 'a bone of Mary Magdalene' drew pilgrims from every part of the Christian world, he became so covetous that he borrowed a knife from his chaplain and tried to cut a bit out of it. When the knife failed him, he bit off two pieces with his own teeth.

Having recalled these grisly associations it would be unjust not to record that at all times there were some in high places who would have nothing to do with such chicanery. Notable among them was Odo of Cluny, who in the tenth century warned that the multiplication of relics and miracles could only bring disgrace to the Church in the long run. Nor were all the religious orders involved in the traffic. Unlike the Benedictines, the Cistercians took little interest in relics. They were too busily engaged in running their estates.

The South-East of England produced more pilgrim shrines than the West for the obvious reason that it was more accessible from the Continent. There were 30 minor shrines in Norfolk alone, and each has left its web of pilgrim ways, however short some of them may be. Essex also is criss-crossed by them. There was a chapel on the Isle of Dogs for pilgrims to give thanks after a safe crossing of the Thames as they made their way from Canterbury to Waltham Holy Cross, and another at West Thurrock for those who were making their way into East Anglia by way of Brentwood, where the place-name, Pilgrims Hatch, is a reminder of the long trail northward to Ely, Walsingham and Bromholm, as well as to Bury St Edmunds. Most of these trails have lost their atmosphere of romance; but we still have the Green Way from Ely to Walsingham, along which we can recapture to the full the spirit of those early pilgrimages, particularly if we travel by night under a full moon.

It seems curious that neither Langland nor Chaucer mention many of these ancient ways. I don't recall more than two in either; yet both have Bromholm in Norfolk, which no-one on casual acquaintance would couple with either Canterbury or Walsingham. Its ruins today stand deserted among nettles and weeds near Bacton on the Norfolk coast, yet in the thirteenth century its 'two transverse pieces of wood of about the size of a man's hand', as its relic has been described, was adored and worshipped as part of the true Cross. After Henry VIII had visited and granted the priory that housed it a festival of three days for the 'Exaltation of the Cross', Bromholm became the centre of a religious cult that was twin to Walsingham, the most aristocratic of English shrines, to which Henry, according to Erasmus, made a pilgrimage, walking the last two miles from Barsham Manor barefoot so that he might express the humility of his devotion by hanging a gold circlet round the neck of 'Our Lady of Walsingham'. Later, alas for such devotion, he was to cause the image of Our Lady to be burned at Chelsea.

13 The Pilgrims' Way near Hollingbourne, Kent, looking east-south-east

CHAPTER FIVE

Packhorse Trails, Drove Roads, and Lost Roads

———◆◆◆———

THE PACKHORSE BRIDGES of Exmoor, the Peak, and the Yorkshire dales, with their low parapets and humped arches continue to fascinate. So they should. They signpost routes that were arteries of trade for a thousand years as surely as ancient barrows signpost the caravan trails of Bronze Age merchants. One of the finest to be seen anywhere is at Bakewell, Derbyshire. In the South of England many of them are still called Galley or Gallox bridges as reminders that the 'galloway', a strong breed of horse of 15 hands or less was found to be ideal for rough country. In the North a packhorse train was often called a jag, and the man in charge of it a jagger, a world that appears in a Yorkshire record for 1379 and is derived from the German *jaeger,* 'hunter'—evidence that like galley it per- petuates the memory of a sturdy breed favoured for the work. There appear to be as many Jagger Lanes in the North as there are Galley Lanes in the South, and jagger in West Yorkshire is still a dialect word for a carter or carrier.

It may well be that the first jaggers were German pedlars who came in at the Yorkshire ports. In course of time many of them would develop a two-way trade, bringing German goods into the country and returning to their homeland with lead from the Yorkshire mines. There is an old packhorse track from Marske in Swaledale to Darlington and Stockton called Jagger Lane.

Packhorse loads were carried in two panniers slung over the saddle, and the reason why the parapets of packhorse bridges are so low is that the train went over the bridge in single-file along a track so narrow that if the parapets had been higher the loaded pan- niers would not have cleared them. To achieve this single-file formation it was important that firm land should lead up to the bridge. That is why so many of them are approached along a raised road called a 'causey', or causeway. These were well maintained, and were often strengthened with stones or paved with flags. The importance of keeping the pack- ways open is shown in the many references in local records to 'pack or prime ways'.

Many packhorse bridges date from the Middle Ages, and are near fords that had hitherto been good enough for cattle crossings and mounted travellers. It was clearly the risk of the valuable merchandise carried by the packhorse trains being swept away and lost while crossing a swollen stream that led to them being built, and determined their design. The humped arches are constructed to allow the heaviest weight of water that might be expected to pass through without endangering the superstructure. Their

14 Holme Packhorse Bridge, Bakewell, Derbyshire

narrowness also contributed to their strength, so where pedestrians might be trapped on longer bridges v-shaped recesses were provided for their safety.

In moorland country several tracks would converge on a single bridge. These might split up on the moors between bridges until on a wide plateau there might be as many as 20 tracks crossing and recrossing. Some of the stone pillars on lonely stretches of moorland, which self-styled archaeologists now 'discover' as phallic symbols in forgotten cults are in fact signposts marking the points where the lines crossed. An admirable book on *Peakland Roads and Trackways,* by A. E. and E. M. Dodd, Moorland Publishing Co, (1974) gives a reliable account of the packhorse trade in what was one of its most important areas of operation. Some of the packways across peat bogs and swamps were given narrow paved causeways when the trade was at its height. Before these were provided conditions must often have been grim. Josiah Wedgwood recalled trains of packhorses that were much too heavily laden being 'hacked' to pieces by the whips of their cruel drivers whilst floundering knee-deep through mud.

Without knowing how completely the villages along the packways depended for their livelihood upon them it is impossible even to imagine the excitement that always attended the arrival of the ponies. On sighting them trotting down the zig-zag track to the bridge to the accompaniment of the tinkling bells of the leader, and the cracking of whips, the entire village would turn out, the farm dogs barking and the children running to the bridge with cries of greeting. All the larger villages along the routes would have alehouses specially favoured by the jaggers, although not all would bear the name. It would not be necessary that they should. The men would know well enough where they could get cheap beds for the night, or straw to lie on in a warm barn while their ponies were turned out on the common. Names like 'The Packsaddle', 'The Packhorses' and 'The Packhorse and Talbot' date from those days, the talbot being the packman's favourite dog.

In towns 'The Woolpack' frequently became the most prosperous local hostelry during the eighteenth century, when all the leading merchants had their own trains of packhorses and sometimes travelled with them. Samuel Smiles relates how a Manchester merchant would send cloth by packhorse over the Derbyshire hills to Nottingham, Lincoln, and Cambridge fairs, returning with wool, malt, and feathers. The merchant himself travelled with the train on horseback, taking orders and settling accounts with golden guineas, 'travelling along bridleways, thro' fields where frequent gibbets warned him of his perils'. The Yorkshire woolmen relied on packhorses to carry their goods to market throughout the eighteenth century. It was estimated that nearly a thousand horsepacks of cotton and woollen goods were brought annually to Stourbridge Fair. The best known name in the transport business today, Pickford, came into prominence in the first half of the seventeenth century, when the firm was founded to carry parcels from Manchester to London. During the following century the packhorse trains on which it relied for more than a hundred years were familiar sights along all the packways of the North; but by that time they were carrying coal, lime, and salt across all the northern counties. The brewing firm of Bass was founded at Stafford about 1720 as a carrier's business delivering parcels by packhorse and selling ale as a sideline.

Kendal was the great packhorse junction in the North of England. In 1752, when the town got its Turnpike Act, trains of galloways went regularly to and from London, Wigan, Whitehaven, Barnard Castle, Penrith, Settle, Cockermouth, Sedbergh, Kirkby Lonsdale, Orton, Dent, and other places, both with general merchandise and with Kendal Green, a coarse drugget nationally acclaimed for wear. From the records of these journeys it is evident that the packhorse trains served rural communities as neither the coach roads nor the railways that succeeded them ever did. The effect of this universal service was that rural industries sprang up in practically every village that had a packhorse bridge, with the mills getting their power from the water that turned their wheels. By this means a simple system of transport was able to sustain a prosperous village economy until, in the nineteenth century, coal began to be produced in sufficient quantity to power the factories built in the new towns of the Industrial Revolution.

Some of these village industries flourished for hundreds of years. Before they fell into decline there were small mills weaving wool in all the Yorkshire dales and cotton in all the Lancashire villages, with housewives spinning at their wheels in all the cottages. Knitting was another village craft. The industry of the 'terrible knitters of Dent' became legendary and was celebrated by the poet Southey among others. In fact, there were knitters producing long stockings in all the cottages and farmhouses in Richmondshire in the time of Elizabeth I, each retaining one as a money bag—hence the phrase: 'She's got a long stocking somewhere'. In Devon there were the paper mills, also powered by water. Few historically minded holiday makers in the West Country can have stood near a ruined mill on the bank of one of the county's fast-flowing streams without wanting to know more about the men who got their living in them, or used them to supplement the living they could scrape from the land.

Perhaps the most impressive of the cottage industries in the Home Counties was chairmaking in the Chilterns, which according to John Saville in *Rural Depopulation of England and Wales, 1851-1951* (1957) provided home employment for 160,000 craftsmen in the 1880s.

Although the railways killed the packhorse trade, freelance packmen continued to be a feature of rural life until the First World War. I remember a packhorse with panniers going daily up and down Whalley Nab in Lancashire, and milk being delivered from fell-side farms in Yorkshire in kits strapped to a pony's back. They were the last survivors along the deserted packways. At the end of the era the pony had been dispensed with, and itinerant Scottish packmen, like the one who inspired the sign of 'The Scotsman's Pack' at Hathersage, carried on the last remnant of the service. Meanwhile Pickfords had put a fleet of vans on the road and Bass had settled for the readier profits of brewing. The last packmen I remember were called Scots drapers. They worked the round of the northern farmhouses with odd articles of clothing and haberdashery in wicker baskets slung over their shoulders on leather straps. Larger articles of clothing were ordered specially and delivered on the next round. In days when farmers' wives seldom went to market they were the bearers of the latest news and gossip, and a resourceful packman would have his own special line in cultivating goodwill. It might be his own remedy for rheumatism, or an ounce of his own 'renowned' tobacco twist for the 'old man' in the chimney corner, which was not only how Bass started the demand for their ale, but how many other world-famous businesses were started. More romantically, the last of the packmen kept alive a traditional sideline that had made the arrival of the packhorse train so eagerly awaited in remote villages for centuries. He was the bearer of messages from a daughter in service in a village a hundred miles away, or a son who was trying to make his fortune in a faraway town. He was also, of course, the successor of the chapman who at church ales, fairs and festivals had sung:

> *Will you buy any tape,*
> *Or lace for your cape,*
> *My dainty duck, my dear —a?*
> *Any silk, any thread,*
> *Any toys for your head,*
> *And the new'st and fin'st wear —a?*

Wordsworth is sometimes ridiculed for having chosen the pedlar as the hero of the *Excursion* by those who have no conception of the romance that surrounded the packmen in rural England before the whole population became mobile.

At a more mundane level the long history of packways is best seen in relation to two of man's most ancient needs: flint and salt. In places like Blackstone Edge in Derbyshire, where flint was worked in Mesolithic times, lime succeeded flint and was carried along the same trackways by lime-gals, yet another name derived from 'galloway'. Other links with the remote past are found in the names of the actual tracks. The Lunedale pack-horse trains were called 'gangs' from the Scandinavian and in the same region—as throughout Cumbria—roads are called 'gates', again from the Scandinavian. But not all 'gals' and 'gates' have this origin. Galgate on the road from Lancaster to Kendal was not the gate, or road, along which the galloway ponies trotted, but the road along which Galway cattle were driven by Irish drovers.

Today the most conspicuous reminders of the lime-gal routes are lime-kilns, most of which date from the eighteenth century and are recognised from the road as mounds of earth with stone archways at the base. These arches were their furnace-holes, sometimes called kindling-holes, into which faggots would be stuffed to ignite the kiln, which was a crucible-shaped well behind the earth walls. This well was packed with alternate layers of coal and limestone to produce the lime used by eighteenth-century 'improvers' as a soil sweetener and manure, and also to make the mortar that is so characteristic of the farm-houses and garden walls in Pennine limestone villages. These kilns went up in thousands across England from Cornwall to Northumberland in the eighteenth century, and every night tramps would be found sleeping on the top of them for the comfort of their warmth. In dry weather narrow tracks can be seen from the air leading from those on the edge of moorland to the farmland on which the lime was spread.

The life of these kilns was short; but they provided one more thread in the tapestry of the English countryside as it can be seen from our old country roads by those who know what to look for. There was little romance, perhaps, in this phase for those who actually lived through it and worked the kilns. But there are always exceptions, and one, surely, was John Clare, the poet, who was a lime-burner at Bridge Casterton at one time. He tells us that he drafted the prospectus for a book of poems while resting on a lime-scuttle. Turner also must be remembered in connection with them. They appear in his sketches and show how much they fascinated him as features of the English landscape.

Easily the most readily identifiable of the old packhorse routes are the saltways, which is not surprising since rock salt did not come into use until 1670, and we have no record of a time when the importance of salt as a preservative was not recognised. Its produc-tion had already started in the Iron Age by the primitive method of pouring sea water over heated stone to obtain a deposit. Later, brine was leached out and boiled to obtain the deposit, and the industry advanced so rapidly from this point that there were 294 salt works in Sussex at Domesday. This was the largest number for any county, and it gave us not only a large number of Sussex saltways but such occupation-names as Waller, which is derived from 'weller', the original name given to a salt-boiler.

The frequency of references to salt in Sussex records makes their absence from those of Hampshire east of Southampton Water the more remarkable. There is not a single reference that I have been able to discover to salt in any of the place-names of the county, and I learn that they are equally absent from its land charters, although Hampshire is a particularly well-chartered county. The explanation must be that the salt from the rich salterns round Southampton Water was carried along the saltways across the unchar-tered New Forest. There must have been scores of salterns—lagoons where salt was produced—along the Solent. We have evidence of this in the fact that at the end of the eighteenth century Lymington ranked only just below Liverpool in importance as a port for the export of salt, collecting in some years as much as £50,000 for the Exchequer in duty. The export from Poole to Canada and the USA continued well into the nineteenth century, when the most important saltway in the New Forest was from Southampton to Lyndhurst, continuing to Burley and Ringwood.

Saltways are found all the way up the east coast of England from the 'red hills' of Essex to the sand dunes of Northumberland, many of which date from pre-Norman times. Forty-five are recorded at Caister in Norfolk alone. Their full development came with the founding of the great abbeys, and continued to figure after the Dissolution in leases stipulating that the tenant should bring in salt by packhorse from the owner's salterns. A favourite story in Westmorland when I was young told how the farmers round Penrith turned this to their personal advantage. Each autumn they would form a packhorse train to collect salt from St Bees on the Cumberland coast, but return with panniers practically empty and explain the deficiency by swearing that the rain had been so heavy that most of the salt had melted and been washed away. The truth was that they had packed into the salt as much smuggled brandy as could be concealed, and had found a hiding place for this before reporting with the salt. After a suitable show of contrition they readily offered to go back the following day for another load. As the landowner's factor was usually privy to the deception, and no doubt in receipt of some of the brandy, the offer was accepted and no-one suffered.

In a countryside as rich as Yorkshire's in religious foundations a powerful abbot might obtain exclusive use of the salterns on the nearest length of coastline, forcing the next to travel long distances for others. As first in the field, the monks of Rievaulx gained for themselves exclusive use of the Teesside salterns and marshes, as well as later appropriating a share of the saltpans at Coatham, near Redcar, along with the abbots of Bylands, Fountains, and Jervaulx. From these the salt was carried along clearly marked saltways, called saltergates, over fords that would be called Salterwath and bridges that would be called Salterbrigg.

Many cross-country Roman roads must have been kept open as saltways—and indeed have served that purpose originally, since the word 'salary' is derived from *salarium*, the allowance made to the legionaries for salt, which must have given rise to the phrase, 'not worth his salt'.

Nowhere can salt have been in greater demand than in the cattle-rearing country of the North, since before feeding-stuffs were introduced for winter diet thousands of cattle were killed off each autumn and salted down. One of the most important saltways in the North follows as nearly as makes no matter the Roman road from Manchester through Ribchester to run through Great Harwood along an ancient track over Whalley Nab to Salthill, Clitheroe. The interesting point is that it suggests that this track predates the moving of the monks from Stanlow in Cheshire to Whalley, because they would bring with them salt rights at Northwich, and so have their own source for distribution over the large area they served when Whalley was one of the largest parishes in Lancashire.

From Whalley one branch of this saltway went up the Hodder Valley to Dunsop Bridge and through the Trough of Bowland to Lancaster and the saltings of Morecambe Bay, where sea-salt was produced at Saltcotes on Wharton Sands. Another branch went from Clitheroe over Waddington Fells to Newton and Slaidburn, and on to join the Hodder Valley trackway in Croasdale, where salt names pick up the trail as the saltway runs down the Roeburn from Salter Fell, through High Salter and Salter to Hornby, Kirkby Lonsdale and Salterwath in Westmorland. It continues over Shap to Penrith, another junction of trackways, with one coming in from Crosby Ravensworth across Salterwath.

But fascinating as these saltways from the coast are, they can seldom be plotted with any degree of accuracy except where they do make use of Roman roads. The case is different with the Midland saltways. Incomparably the most important of these were those from Droitwich in Worcestershire, and Northwich, Middlewich, and Nantwich in Cheshire, which became so important when rock-salt superseded sea-salt. Fortunately, Worcestershire, which was culturally backward in the Middle Ages, was an ecclesiastical county and therefore rich in records. And both Worcestershire and Cheshire have been exceptionally well served by local antiquaries and historians who have painstakingly explored the saltways of the Midlands and published their findings in the Proceedings of learned societies. These show that salt pans were owned over vast areas by the abbots, and after the Dissolution by the owners of historic estates in the 'Dukeries'.

The valuable salt pans at Droitwich came into multiple ownership, with interests as far away as Princes Risborough in Oxfordshire. After the Dissolution the Cheshire wicks became commercial ventures, with salt for sale to anyone with money to pay for it or goods to barter. One of the main saltways from the Midlands ran over Blackstone Edge to carry salt into Yorkshire. Although when hill country was reached the saltways could follow existing tracks, including Roman roads, in parts of the heavily wooded regions of Worcestershire and Warwickshire they were to become the basis of a new road system in many areas, which if pre-Norman must have been welcomed by the Saxons as more adaptable to their way of life than Roman roads normally were. .

Drove Roads

Drove roads, the other important long-distance trackways, served the less complex purpose of providing through-ways for livestock and are to be distinguished from packhorse ways by their width. Whereas packhorse trails were no wider than was required by horses trotting along them in single file, drove roads were 40 to as much as 90 feet wide. Both reached their peak in the eighteenth century.

The supreme portrait of the Scottish drover in literature is Sir Walter Scott's Rob Roy, or 'Red Robert', which is not surprising since Sir Walter's own grandfather had been a drover in the days when Scots drovers were really cattle dealers, who bought the cattle before starting the drive, in contrast to the Welsh drovers who usually travelled as agents for the owners. Sir Walter again portrayed the background to droving in his introduction to the tale of the *Two Drovers,* and in *Guy Mannering,* where a hedge alehouse near Gilsland is described as a favourite haunt of drovers and farmers 'in their way to and from the trysts in Cumberland, and especially those who came from Scotland'. These trysts were fairs to which gangs of drovers, as the term is commonly understood, brought herds of up to 200 head of cattle, with one drover and two dogs to every 40 beasts.

From these fairs the cattle were driven south to the great marts north of London, like the one on Wanstead Flats, before being sold at Smithfield, halting for the night in the shelter of grassy hollows called 'stances'. Many of these can be identified near old inns by the way the roadside verges expand to double their normal width to provide grazing for the cattle while the drover, after refreshing himself in the inn or alehouse wrapped his plaid about him and settled down for the night under the hedge, with his dog to guard him. Further evidence of the use of a particular piece of roadside waste as a stance would be the presence of a stream where the cattle could water. Some of these old stances have now been enclosed; but they can still be identified where present-day hedgerows come up to the carriageway, if a short distance behind them there is a continuous hedgerow with old trees and flowering shrubs indicating the original line.

The droving of large herds of cattle to London and provincial cities started before the Dissolution. There is evidence of droving as early as the fourteenth century, and from the sixteenth drovers, like corn-badgers, had to be licensed. These licenses were only granted to married men who were householders and more than 30 years of age, which indicates that the old-time drover was a very different type of man from the loafers who hung about cattle marts 60 or 70 years ago, to pick up the few coppers they needed for a drink or a bed in the local doss-house in return for driving two or three beasts to a farm a few miles away, leaving the farmer free for a crack with his cronies and a seat at the farmers' 'ordinary', as the market-day mid-day meal at the 'local' was called. Droving in its great days was an occupation of trust, which is obvious if we consider the value of the cattle being driven along the roads, and the temptations to which drovers would be subjected. All along the routes there would be unscrupulous characters ready to ply them with liquor and dump their bodies in a convenient copse before driving off the cattle. Every market town had its stories of murders of both farmers and drovers waylaid in lonely places. Consequently, several of them would usually arrange to travel together.

There were two main systems of drove roads, one for Scots, the other for Welsh cattle. The Welsh especially made use of the prehistoric ridgeways, enlivening them with fairs like the one at Weyhill, near Andover. It would be at such a fair that Michael Henchard in *The Mayor of Casterbridge* sold his wife. The name Mauthway in north Hampshire is derived from the Welsh word for sheep, and seems to come from the same root as mutton. Between them these two systems brought 100,000 head of cattle and 750,000 sheep to Smithfield annually. Now Smithfield is deprived of its former glory; but whenever I pass through its arcades I recall the scene described by Dickens in *Oliver Twist*, with 'the thick steam perpetually rising from the reeking bodies of the cattle and mingling with the fog'.

Before being driven into London for sale at Smithfield bullocks had to be fattened up after the rigours of their long trek, and in counties within a few days' reach of London commons and marshes were the most favoured feeding grounds, the best being along the coastal plain of Sussex in the South and the Norfolk marshes in the East. From Sussex the cattle were driven through such towns as Storrington and Steyning along roads, now for the most part green lanes, converging on gaps in the Downs, with Findon Gap the most popular. One drove road in Sussex that can still be followed links Amberley with Rackham and continues to Wisborough Green. John Byng encountered 'vast droves'

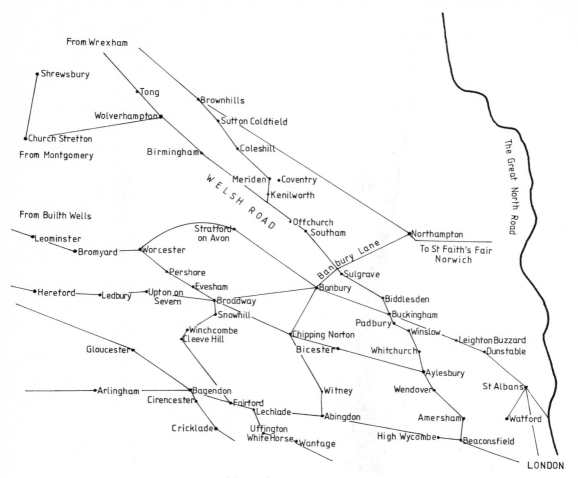

Map 6   Drove roads from Wales

making their way from the Sussex marshes through Horsebridge. Unpaved roads were favoured wherever available because they were less harmful to the animals' feet. This is noticeable near Billinghurst, where the drove road, like the local drift-ways, runs parallel to the Roman Stane Street. The importance of this protection is appreciated when it is found that even where conditions for droving were at their best it was unusual for cattle to be driven more than 12 miles a day.

The organisation of drives could not be casually undertaken. There was too much at stake for that, both in money and livestock. A Welsh drover named David Jones found the answer to the money problem in 1799 by founding the Black Ox Bank; but not everyone was willing to entrust his money to a banker in those days. The Sir Watkin Williams-Wynn of the day employed a drover named David Lloyd for 50 years and entrusted him with several thousand pounds at a time to pay his London debts. Drovers with that kind of money on them must have been well armed. Nor was their courage their only characteristic. There were scholars among them, meditating on solemn

15 Typical marker stone on a drovers' road out of Wales

matters as they lay under the stars at night. Four Welsh drovers figure in the list of sub-
scribers to Dr. Johnson's Dictionary, which reminds us that Dr. Johnson's idea of
happiness was to be driven rapidly in a post-chaise with a pretty woman, so it belongs to
the romantic credit of the road, although his comment on the drovers making their way
south from Scotland would probably have been cynical rather than romantic.

Several of the drove roads on the Welsh border converge on Clyro below the Black
Mountains, the village to which Francis Kilvert, the diarist who was invariably
romantic, went as curate in 1865. 'The Feathers' at Ledbury was a famous drovers' inn,
with a field behind it for the cattle to rest in before being driven over the Malvern Hills,
and on through Little Malvern and Welland, where the wide grass verges are typical of
such a road, to cross the Severn at Upton and go on to Broadway. There the wide street
is again typical of a halt on a drove road, with greens for the cattle to graze on before
being driven up the hill to Stow-on-the-Wold or Moreton-in-Marsh; but it is difficult
now to imagine the luxuriously appointed 'Lygon Arms' as ever having been a drovers'

inn, which in its humbler days it was. But then Broadway is in every respect a different place from that described by Thomas Habington in Stuart times as 'the Broad and highe waye from the Shepherds' coates which on the mounted woldes shelter themselfes under hylles from the rage of stormes downe to the most fruytfull vale of Evsham'.

The journey from Scotland was more arduous and fraught with greater dangers than the journey from Wales can ever have been. 'Gearstones Inn', near Ribblehead (rebuilt in the 1880s), one of the best know drovers' inns in the Pennine country, was described by John Byng,[*] who visited it in 1792, as 'the seat of misery', yet crammed with Scots cattle dealers in plaids and kilts, the heath in front of it thronged with Scots cattle and drovers. At Ingleton he again noted 'vast droves' of Scottish cattle passing to the South. The Pennines are criss-crossed by old drove roads, some of which retain such names as 'Driving Road', now a green lane round Dent Fell, or Galloway Gate, the name of the old main road out of Dentdale into Mallerstang. Defoe reported, probably without exaggeration, that it was 'no uncommon thing for a Galloway nobleman to send 4,000 sheep and 4,000 head of cattle to England in a year, and sometimes much more'. Among literary references to drovers none is more delightful than Dorothy Wordsworth's noting of 'little Scotch cattle' grazing on the pastures below the Hambleton Hills. They would be travelling along the Bronze Age track that mounted the Cleveland Hills at Scarth Nick after crossing the Tees near Yarm, to continue along a ridgeway over Osmotherley Moor to reach eventually Cooper Cross at the head of Sutton Bank. It would be along this green road that old Mr Jorrocks 'encountered a large drove of Scotch kyloes picking their way as they went'.

This road was favoured not only because it avoided the rough roads of Yorkshire that were then notorious for being surfaced with loose sharp stones that could cripple a beast; but also because it bypassed turnpikes. After passing through Laurence Sterne's Coxwold, however, it had to join the Great North Road in the end, although without doubt the Turnpike Trusts extended the use of green roads—they were hardly lanes— long after the coach roads had been metalled. On reaching the highway, the drovers made their way to cattle farriers, some of whom did lively business shoeing cattle. One at Langthorpe, near Boroughbridge, claimed that he went through 30,000 special nails used in shoeing bullocks during the course of a year. Some smiths boasted that they could shoe 70 beasts a day. As 30,000 cattle a year were said to pass through Wetherby that also must have been a prosperous town for shoeing smiths, yet comparatively few of these shoes, called 'cucs' or 'kews', are dug up in the countryside—perhaps because they were made in two parts to fit cloven hoofs, so are not recognised for what they are. As in so many fields of North Country research, the man to go to when in search of information about the drove roads of the North is Arthur Raistrick, whose *Green Roads on the Pennines* is an invaluable guide.

One of the greatest cattle dealers using these roads was Ralph Robb of Topcliffe, near Thirsk, who in the early years of the nineteenth century travelled to Falkirk Fair with £30,000 in Bank of England notes in his wallet, and returned with 12,000 head of cattle, having drawn bills for the balance of their price.[†] But the king of the cattle country in the

*Torrington Diaries, 111, p.58
† *A Family History: The Wyndhams of Norfolk and Somerset,* vol. 11, p.304

North was John Birtwhistle of Skipton, who fattened his stock in the Great Close of Malham Moor during the second half of the eighteenth century. This grazing ground was a vast enclosure of 732 acres, in which as many as 5,000 head of cattle could be grazing at any one time. It was estimated that in addition to those in the Great Close, Birtwhistle might often have as many as 10,000 head of cattle somewhere on the drove roads.

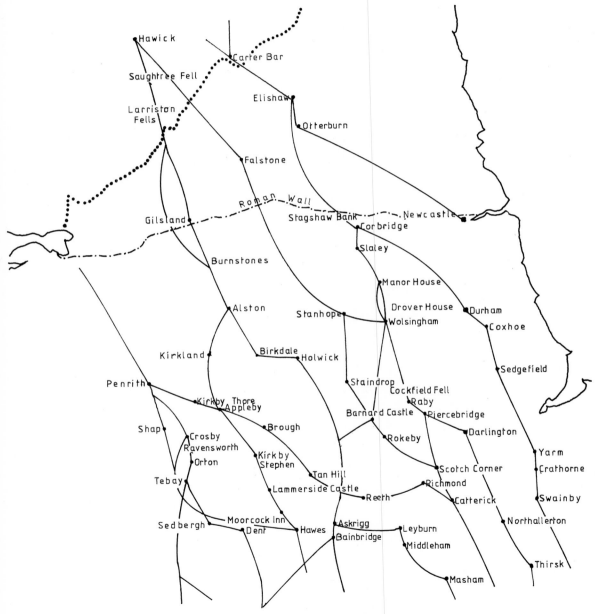

Map 7   Drove roads from Scotland

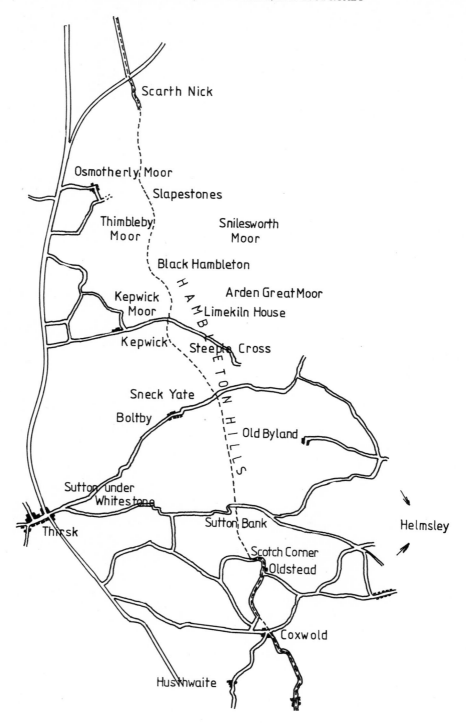

Map 8   The Hambleton Drove Road

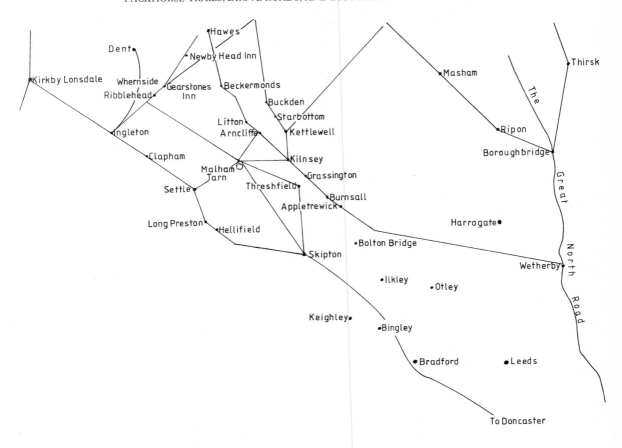

Map 9   Drove roads in Yorkshire

This droving business could not fail to have its effect on dairy farming in the dales, and because there were no large towns within reach for the daily distribution of milk in those days, Yorkshire became famous for its cheeses. These were sold in the markets of Settle, Skipton, Hawes, Richmond, Bishop Auckland, and Barnard Castle, while the butter was collected by higglers and sold to grocers.

Its wide grass verges, which made the Great North Road so much more attractive than other main roads, were obviously due to its use as a drove road. There are no accurate figures of the number it carried, but it is claimed that at the height of the droving business 2,000 cattle passed through Boroughbridge daily. However, when careful counts were made at Wetherby Bridge in 1779 from 6 August to 25 November, the total number was 21,248, which although more than 1,300 weekly makes the Boroughbridge claim more than a little inflated. Some of the farmers who let out fields for travelling flocks and herds planted small clumps of Scotch firs near their farmhouses as signs that they had pasture to let, and were well disposed towards Scots.

After being fattened on the Norfolk marshes many Scots cattle were sold at St Faith's Fair, north of Norwich, the largest fair in England for Scots drovers; but some made the extra 120 miles to London. Others sold their cattle and returned to Scotland, leaving the Norfolk drovers to distribute from St Faith's. One of these, a drover named Tom Denny, used to drive cattle to London, then return home by coach, leaving his dog to make the return journey on foot.

In the middle of the eighteenth century the roads out of East Anglia got a new kind of traffic. It was found that by driving them first through tar and then through sand, geese acquired 'boots' in which they could travel as far as London if need be. So as many as 2,000 might be encountered in a single drive, to be sold in 'goose-yards' in towns like Epping. These drives were always started in late August, when the harvest was in, and the geese could be fed on the stubble as they travelled. They continued to be driven along these roads for approximately two months—that is to say, until the roads became too muddy for their short legs and clumsy feet. Geese were also driven from the Fens westward to be sold at the great Goose Fair at Nottingham. As for turkeys, it is estimated that 150,000 of them would be driven over Stratford Bridge on the Stour, while from West Suffolk almost as many would be driven over Newmarket Heath and down the A11 road.

Nor were these the only forms of livestock on roads in days when their life was so much more colourful than it is now. Droves of calves were to be met with on the roads out of Dorset and Somerset into Devon for sale at Exeter. Pigs were driven along hogways—of which Pig Street in Axminster is a reminder. Bristol had a flourishing market for pigs driven in from Wales. Perhaps the drove roads of the South come to life most vividly in *Our Village,* where Mary Russell Mitford writes: 'That apparently lonely and trackless common is the very high road of the drovers who came from different points of the West to the great mart, London. Seldom would that green be found without a flock of Welsh sheep, footsore and weary, and yet tempted into grazing by the short fine grass dispersed over its surface, or a drive of gaunt Irish pigs, sleeping in a corner, or a score of Devonshire cows straggling in all directions, picking the long grass from the surrounding ditches; whilst dog and man, shepherd and drover, might be seen basking in the sun'.

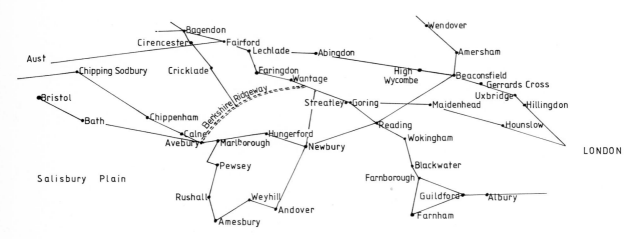

Map 10   Downland drove roads

The Lost Roads

If we think only of their uses, most of the roads we have discussed in this chapter might be described as 'lost', even if they are now being rediscovered as long distance footpaths. Whenever we stumble into one that has now become a blind lane we may get something of the feeling Kipling expressed so nostalgically in the poem beginning:

> *They shut the road through the woods*
> *Seventy years ago. . .*

In another poem Kipling reminds us of roads that were favoured because they were lost: prehistoric trackways that had become overgrown and abandoned, so were ideal for smugglers because their springy turf provided silent trails along which illicit liquor could be smuggled in, to be picked up on lonely heaths where might be seen:

> *Five and twenty ponies,*
> *Trotting through the dark—*
> *Brandy for the parson,*
> *'Baccy for the Clerk;*
> *Laces for a Lady, letters for a spy,*
> *And watch the walls, my darling, while*
> *the Gentlemen go by.*

The Peddars Way, which ran from the Norfolk coast to Sussex, must have been the longest of these smugglers' roads, which in parts acquired such names as the 'Kegway', found on Romney Marsh. Trackways like the ridgeway from the Hampshire coast at Lymington to Burley, which was used for smuggling cloth out of the country and brandy in, continued to be watched for illegal entry of one sort or another until the nineteenth century. Those who used it for the clandestine export of wool were called 'owlers' because they worked by night.

The New Forest is a happy hunting ground for anyone interested in landscape as a palimpsest of rural records. In contrast to what has happened where the land has been cultivated, we can see there how tracks first used by invaders were later used by smugglers, and what enormous advantages the region had for both. At Lymington there is still a peninsular site cut off by a bank and ditch, at Buckland a triple-banked camp called 'Buckland Rings', and at Exbury, at the mouth of Beaulieu River, another peninsular earthwork. All tracks would eventually converge on Winchester, with Cadnam as the local rallying place on the east and Ringwood on the west. The importance of these routes is shown by the way they are signposted, as it were, by earthworks like Burley Castle and Castle Malwood.

Picket Post must always have been a splendid sighting point for those on both sides of the law. For those keeping watch in prehistoric times it could be used to signal enemy approaches to Castle Malwood, from which a beacon could flash the alarm inland, while 2,000 years later less public methods of signalling alarms could be used. I never walk along Captain's Row at Lymington without longing to know more about the men who lived in those tall houses, many of whom must have grown rich during the most

profitable period of smuggling, which must surely have been while cloth from Ringwood was being exchanged for liquor smuggled in from France. Many of these cargoes
would be rowed upstream to Boldre and carried from there to Brockenhurst. The present
main roads through the Forest suggest little of this illegal use. They are much too direct.
But the old road from Brockenhurst to Minstead, the mother parish and ancient centre,
would have many tales to tell if secrecy had not been such a vital part of their value.
Similarly the A31, although it runs along the line of the old ridgeway past Picket Post
means little; but we can regain the spirit of the past if we leave it to cross Milkham
Enclosure and Slufter's Enclosure to Bramble Hill, where the old ridgeway turns north-
west to run along the B3078 for a short distance, leaving it where it bends round to
Fordingbridge, and eventually to reach Pepperbox on the Wiltshire border.

Perhaps the most intriguing lost road in the New Forest is the King's Lane along
which the body of William Rufus was carried in a cart to Winchester by Purkis, the
charcoal burner, after the fatal shot by an arrow near Stoney Cross. The original track,
now lost, must have run from Canterton to Cadnam, and from there through Copy-
thorne, Nursling, Chandlers Ford and Otterbourne—in short, along the Old Sarum
Road, which has now been bypassed.

One reminder of the New Forest smugglers is the tower of Kinson church, just off the
Wimborne to Christchurch road, which has a broken ledge half way up its squat tower, said
to have been damaged by kegs of brandy being clumsily hoisted into the belfry. A tomb
near the church door is alleged to have had one side hinged so that liquor could be stored
in it; but it is hard to believe that this could have been more than a very temporary hiding
place. Better evidence that Kinson was a smugglers' cache is the gravestone of Robert
Trotman, 'who was barbarously murder'd on the shore, near Poole, 24th March, 1765'.

> *A little tea, one leaf I did not steal,*
> *For guiltless bloodshed I to God appeal;*
> *Put tea in one scale, Human Blood in t'other,*
> *And think, what 'tis to slay thy harmless brother.*

Robert Trotman did at all events get a Christian burial. Grimmer reminders of what
happened to law-breakers who were caught are found all over England in names that
perpetuate the memory of the gallows that once stood near them. Probably not one in a
million of the London commuters who drive past Gallows Corner in south-west Essex
daily thinks of the significance of the name, yet the gallows are clearly depicted on old
maps. Many of these names have now been euphemised to Gallastree, Gallasfield, or
Gallantry.

Vast stretches of moorland are similarly scored with the remains of lost roads, and for
the same reason, that the moors, like the New Forest, have remained uncultivated. The
most haunted of these are what are called Lykeways in the South—lyke meaning body
—and Corpseways in the North. The need for these long trackways along which the dead
had to be carried for burial was that only parish churches were allowed to have
graveyards. So where parishes were as large as those on Dartmoor or in Cumbria the
dead might have to be carried 20 miles or more. There was neither hearse nor carriages
in these funeral processions. The bodies were borne in coffins strapped to a horse's back,

*16 Peddars Way,
running
south-east from
Fring, Norfolk*

followed by mourners either walking or on horseback, the women riding pillion. It is not surprising that winter deaths were dreaded, and that it was cause for thanksgiving, not regret that an ailing relative 'lived all winter and died in spring'.

The most gruesome of these corpseways was the one through Swindale and Keld to the graveyard at Shap, which from Hawes reservoir to Mardale Common is called The Old Corpse Road. Relief came when a burial ground was allowed at Mardale in 1729, but was lost again in what might be thought harrowing circumstances when the reservoir submerged the church and a hundred bodies were exhumed from the graveyard to be reburied at Shap. Fortunately by that time there were better means of reaching a place of burial than along the Corpse Road.

As this track ran through a countryside still farmed by descendents of the Norsemen who settled there a thousand years ago, superstitions and legends grew up round mishaps that occurred on these often far from pious occasions. If a horse bolted for no apparent reason an unnatural death, either in the farmhouse from which the cortege started, or on the lonely fells surrounding it was suspected. If the horse cast the coffin before bolting, a violent death at the hands of a jealous or covetous member of the deceased's family was believed to be indicated and wicked gossip circulated. Some of the horses never were recaptured by the family, but were said to be seen galloping across the fells like restless spirits during storms, a superstition that may not be thought incredible in this kind of country, if it is remembered how prominently the horse figures in Norse folklore.

Another corpseway that retains its name runs out of Grinton under Harkerside Moor. Two others in Yorkshire that I have walked are the one running through Swaledale, which must be eight miles long, and the one at the western end of Wensleydale, which can be identified at the back of the Moorcock Inn. Some of these corpseways were actually church-ways, which could be several miles long in parishes that included several 'townships'.

The more intensive cultivation of land in the South has obliterated most of the corpse-ways; but several survive in footpaths and green lanes, even in built-up towns. An especially interesting one runs from Forest side to Chingford old church through modern housing estates, yet is maintained along its entire course as either a footpath or a bridleway. At Leatherhead in Surrey there is a tradition that one penny was formerly charged to carry a corpse through the Swan Brewery yard.

Moorland tracks that may well puzzle even the next generation are recognized by older countryfolk immediately as peat-ways. Sixty years ago peat-cutting for winter fuel was an annual event in the North of England. The peat was cut from the mosses on the fell tops and brought down on sledges that were steered by hand along tracks that cut zig-zag furrows down the fellsides. In the North this practically died out during the Second World War. It continues on a commercial scale in the West of England, but not for fuel. In my boyhood there were many inns and farmhouses on the northern fells in which it was claimed that the peat fires had burned continuously since the houses were built 300 years earlier. I remember especially an inn at Blubberhouses, near Whitby, where this was claimed. As there was no artificial means of obtaining heat for either hot water or cooking in those days these claims could not be disputed. I have read somewhere that peat cutting was restarted using modern methods at Witherslack, near the foot of

Windermere, soon after the end of the war. I don't know whether it continues or not.

Other names of lost roads, such as sandways, rushways, ironways, leadways and tinways are self-explanatory. A road across Cleveland Plain is called Ladgate Lane as a reminder that lead from the Pennine mines was carried along it through Catterick to Guisborough. The origin of such names in open country is clear enough; but where they are found in towns they point to lost roads as surely as do Packhorse Close or Sumpters Yard, a name that always delights me at St Albans. Perhaps the commonest are names incorporating Causeway, Carsey, or Carsel, indicating lost roads across areas that have now been drained but were formerly marshland. And the number of farm-names containing a reference to local swamp or wet land is evidence of how much of the country did remain undrained until the eighteenth century.

The North has many names of Scandinavian origin that are unknown in the South. An 'outrake' is a sheep track along which the sheep were brought down from the fells at lambing time, or for shearing. Another local road-name in the North is Tram-road: a road formed of beams to form a continuous trackway—a corduroy road. There is a 1555 reference to repairing the 'highway or tram' in the Barnard Castle records, and one dated 1650 to 'tram lands' in the records of Kirkby Lonsdale in Westmorland. This lost name for a road of beams or tree trunks split down the middle is perpetuated in the track along which tram-rails were laid, and was later transferred to the cars that ran on them. Allied to this name is Stump Road, a road formed of tree stumps. And one that I am always expecting to find but never do is 'Broggers way', a word that appears to be the origin of broker, but might have come into use when a 'brogger' was a licensed pedlar in wool. If it did it would have to be distinguished from a brog-way, which is a road marked out by brogs, or tree stumps driven into marshes. In Essex we have the Broomway, so called because it was marked by broom stakes across Maplin Sands from Wakering Stairs to Fisherman's Head.

The most famous road marked out by brogs was the 14-mile-long road which crossed Morecambe Bay from Ulverston to Hest Bank and saved travellers making the long journey round the Bay. The shifting channels of the Leven, Kent, and Keer rivers made the employment of guides for the crossing essential in bad weather; but for a very long time it was reasonably negotiable during the summer months, although this can never have been without risk since the parish registers of Cartmel record many instances of 'death by drowning on the Sands'! Before the Dissolution the monks of Furness provided a guide mounted on a white horse to conduct travellers and pilgrims across the Sands to the abbey. He was called The Carter, and Carter House and Carter Lane preserve his memory.

CHAPTER SIX

Trackways to Turnpikes

WE KNOW that the dexterity of the natives in handling their war chariots astonished the Romans when they attempted to land in 55BC and made that first invasion abortive. We also know that tin from the Cornish mines was carried by two-wheeled carts to the sea for export at an early date, because Pliny found them so efficient that he purchased one for use in Italy. How then do we explain the slowness in bringing vehicular transport into general use? Undoubtedly the answer is the neglect that valley roads suffered throughout so many centuries following the Roman withdrawal.

Carts would continue to be used along well-drained ridgeways; they would come to grief when swamps had to be crossed. There was also the question of personal ease. Until either leather suspension straps or metal springs had been invented the back of a horse, with its built-in muscles, was more comfortable than a cart for a long journey, and baggage was more conveniently carried by trains of packhorses than by lumbering waggons because there was less jolting. So Chaucer's abbess rode side-saddle, his burgess's wife astride, and most wives pillion. Even judges rode on horseback until this was no longer thought dignified, and when they took to using coaches their arrival for assizes became much more problematical than it had been. Nevertheless, we know that King John's baggage was in waggons and carts when it was lost in the Wash, and that even when the body of St Edmund was being carried back to St Edmundsbury it arrived at the little Saxon church at Greensted in a cart.

In view of this confused evidence there is no point in discussing how numerous carts were in the Middle Ages. Common sense tells us that they would not replace the horse for either personal use or the transport of baggage in most parts of the country, and that waggon-ways and packhorse trails would continue together. What we do know, however, is that the dissolution of the monasteries put an end to what at one time had appeared to be an inexhaustible source of revenue for the maintenance of roads and bridges, and that these were at their worst during the Tudor and Stuart periods. The bishops who succeeded the abbots did their best to encourage benefactions; but they lacked the power to inspire the fear the abbots had inspired by the threat of excommunication, and on the whole they had little success.

But the collapse of the old order did not happen overnight. There had been a general degeneration of monastic life for the best part of a century before Henry VIII sent the abbots packing. His father, Henry VII, in his will directed that £2,000 should be spent on the repair of the highways and bridges between Windsor and Richmond, and from there to Southwark, Greenwich, and Canterbury. This was a main road. At that time few minor roads in the London area were paved. The first was the ancient hollow way called Holloway, which was given a stone foundation in 1417. It was an interesting choice because it shows that when roads suitable for wheeled transport came to be constructed, even in the London area, they were along the old packhorse tracks with gradients so steep that, however negotiable they had been for ponies with panniers strapped to their backs, would require extra horses to get waggons and carts up them.

London clay was to present its own peculiar problems for more than two centuries after the Dissolution. Where roads had a stone foundation the problems were more readily solved. Yet Richard Bellasis, who was in charge of the dismantling of Jervaulx Abbey in 1537, which although on low ground was near stone, wrote that he could not dispatch the lead from the roofs until the following summer because the ways were so foul that no carriage could pass along them in winter. This was in Yorkshire, where the abbeys had been exceptionally strong and wealthy; but it suggests that the loss of civil power was also a factor that had contributed to the neglect of highways, particularly in the North, where the Wars of the Roses had undermined the manorial system and feudal obligations had been neglected.

As the result of various factors producing a cumulative effect, both civil and ecclesiastical power were at a low ebb when the Tudors reached the throne and a 'catch as catch can' attitude developed. Just as the Roman remains had served as quarries to be raided at the withdrawal of the legions, the abbeys were ransacked at the dissolution of the monasteries, and such road repairing as was undertaken was at their expense. They were destroyed without scruple along with the wayside crosses, which were broken up to repair market-ways — their large blocks packed in and surfaced with small stones raked from the fields and pebbles dredged from the streams. When these were not available, heather and faggots would be cut from the moors and packed with mud.

The general attitude is well illustrated in a story told by G. G. Coulton in *Mediaeval Panorama* (1943) about a Leighton Buzzard glover, who while returning home from Aylesbury market just before Christmas 1499, fell into a pit in the middle of the highway and was drowned. This pit, which measured eight feet by ten on the surface and was eight feet deep, had been dug during the day by the servants of an Aylesbury miller named Richard Boose, to obtain 'ramming clay' for the repair of his mill. As it had quickly filled with water from the winter rain, the pit had become indistinguishable from the rest of the highway in the dusk and the glover had been given no warning of the danger ahead. The miller was charged with causing the death of the glover, but was acquitted on the defence that he had no malicious intent in having the pit dug. His sole purpose in ordering his servants to dig it was to obtain clay for the repair of his mill, and he did not know of any other place where he could obtain the kind of clay he needed.

To understand such an attitude we need to bear in mind that roads were still regarded as no more than rights of passage for transport and mounted travellers. There was a strong bias against any form of vehicular traffic until well into the sixteenth century and in most places until well into the seventeenth. This did not, of course, apply to the glover of Leighton Buzzard, whose case would appear to be extreme on any argument; but all long-distance travellers were regarded as a curse by local farmers, who suffered from horsemen straying from the roads when these became impassable, just as ramblers in the twentieth century are sometimes guilty of straying from marked footpaths for the same reason. At the Dissolution less than half the lowland country would have been enclosed, despite the spread of pasture farming.

Thomas Tusser complains about this trespassing in his *Hundred Good Points of Husbandry* (1557):

> *What footpaths are made, and how broad,*
> *Annoyance too much to be borne;*
> *With horse and with cattle, what road*
> *Is made through every man's corn?*

When this crossing of fields was by carts and waggons it was all the more grievous, because the farmers themselves would bring in most of their crops on sledges, as they continued to do on northern fells until our own day. Even on the made-up roads waggons were then viewed much as we view juggernauts.

There was yet another factor operating against adequate road repair in coastal counties: the fear of invasion. This was especially strong in Sussex, where the landowners argued that the bad condition of the roads was defensive, and paid little heed to farmers who complained about the difficulty in getting their produce to market. So for one reason or another the roads in Tudor England were already in a parlous condition, and little was done to improve them. Acts of Parliament might be passed for the repair of major roads, like the one passed during Mary Tudor's reign for the repair of the causeway between Bristol and Bath; but they were few and largely ineffective.

Fear of invasion was probably a more widespread factor in the South and East of England than we imagine. It was partly to allay this fear that a comprehensive system of beacon warning signals was established during the reign of Henry VIII. Such a system had, in fact, existed in a primitive form since the time of Alfred the Great. The Tudor measure provided for a much more efficient system to be instituted based on three lines of beacons, the first covering the coastline, the second on hills a few miles inland, and the third on chosen vantage points seen over large inland areas. The siting was remarkably well and significantly chosen. The coastal line became the stations used by coastguards on the look-out for smugglers; the second line was remarkable for its approximation to the old 'castle' sites, and the third, although happily serving a less permanent use, brought the whole country within immediate alert if an enemy threatened to land. All were provided with barrels of tar and flax for igniting it, mounted on massive squat baulks of timber called Beacon Trees. The system was so impressive in its coverage that in Edward VI's reign the Spanish ambassador —the man it was most necessary to impress—reported that 'by means of beacons the English say they can muster twenty-five to thirty thousand men in two hours'. The claim was excessive; but there was sufficient truth in it to make a brave show of strength when the Armada sailed up the Channel.

Meanwhile inland travel increased and the inns that had replaced the monastic hospices were often as much pits for the unwary as the one the Bedfordshire glover had stumbled into so fatally. Tapsters and ostlers everywhere were on the look-out for travellers showing signs of wealth or carelessness in their cups.

Within a generation of the Dissolution conditions on the roads had already become so intolerable that Parliament was compelled to assume responsibility for—in the words of the 1555 Act—'amending of highways being now very noisome and tedious to travel in and dangerous to all passengers and carriages'. This historic Highway Act remained in force for nearly 300 years, although not very effectively. Its basic weakness was that although it was a national Act it made roads a parish responsibility under the lords of the manors and the local Justices, and this experiment in devolution proved to be as ineffective when it came to enforcement as many of its successors have been.

The Act provided that two parishioners should be elected at a parish session each year to act as Highway Surveyors, or Waywardens, to inspect roads, water-courses, bridges, and pavements within their parish three times a year and report on what they found deficient. Their concern was with the highways exclusively. The byways were left to the care of the landowners. From the outset the office was unpopular, which meant that the cunning ones always contrived to avoid being elected, and as the persons who were elected had neither local popularity nor technical knowledge of road maintenance, their reports were simple in the extreme, and like the approved answers to Parliamentary questions told the questioner nothing that he did not already know.

Under the 1555 Act every person holding land of an annual value of £50 or more, either arable or pasture, was required to supply two able-bodied men, with a team of either oxen or horses, and tools or implements for the work of repairing the highways for eight hours on four consecutive days annually, which in 1563 was increased to six days, and the surveyors were authorised to dig out sufficient gravel for the work without paying for it. Cottagers without land were required either to work themselves or find substitutes.

The main faults in this well-intentioned Act were that it failed to specify the standard of maintenance to be aimed at and offered no incentives that might have attracted unwilling labour. Consequently, our Essex country parson, William Harrison of Rad-winter, who travelled tirelessly along the main roads of England for his *Description of the Island of Britain,* prefaced to Holinshed's *Chronicles* (1577), wrote: 'The rich do so cancel their portions, and the poor so loiter in their labours that of all the six scarcely two good days' work are performed', and some of the work that was done was not 'upon those ways that lead from market to market, but each Surveyor ammendeth such byplots and lanes as seem best for his own commodity and more easy passage unto his fields and pastures'. Two hundred years later—in 1763 to be precise—Sir John Hawkins, in his *Observations on the State of the Highways,* wrote that in the few parishes where the Statute was maintained the labourers treated the days as holidays from their regular employment and spent the time in riot and drunkenness.

In Tudor times feelings ran much higher between neighbouring parishes than they do now, and a newly appointed Surveyor would be careful not to be drawn into disputes as to which was responsible for the repair of a highway that ran along a parish boundary—and nearly every parish had such roads. These disputes usually arose as a result of the failure of the Act to define responsibilities adequately, although in fairness it should be added that Parliament would have found it difficult to do so because before the Dissolution land in adjoining parishes would frequently belong to the abbot of a single large foundation, who would have made provision for the maintenance of the highways in the manner described in a previous chapter. However, when boundary disputes arose the local Solomons were inclined to rule that the county boundary ran down the middle of a provocatively chosen highway, and land charters usually confirmed the judgment. It was about as helpful in maintaining public order as the custom adopted by the West Suffolk police after race meetings at Newmarket, of getting rid of the drunks by driving them on to the other side of the High Street, where they became the responsibility of the Cambridgeshire police because this was one of the best known highway county boundaries.

Many of these boundary disputes continued for centuries. Probably the most acrimonious arose when highways were diverted for the greater convenience of long-distance travellers. There was certainly more than a little local difficulty along the borders of Hertfordshire with both Middlesex and Essex when the Old North Road was first diverted. In all these diversion disputes the local people felt aggrieved because the old line had long been accepted for local needs, which had adapted themselves to it, and they felt cheated when they were required to maintain new roads constructed for the benefit of people from distant parts who were a nuisance to them anyway.

The present B1368 road from Puckeridge through Braughing to Cambridge ran into trouble when it crossed county boundaries. The section through Barley Bottom was found to be in Essex and therefore the responsibility of the Essex parishes through which it passed, and not of the neighbouring parishes in either Hertfordshire or Cambridgeshire. But as Essex had no interest in it, and the main beneficiaries of the road were the Cambridge colleges it served in a variety of ways, it remained in wretched condition until the Master and Fellows of Trinity Hall generously made funds available for its repair pending a new settlement being reached between the trustees of the Cambridge and Wadesmill Turnpikes.

The sixteenth century produced three important authoritative eye-witness accounts of travel in England: Leland's *Itinerary,* Harrison's *Description,* and Camden's *Britannia,* in that order; but only Harrison's has much to say about roads. Even the cartographers showed little interest in them until the last decade of the sixteenth century, and when at last distances were shown they were computed, not measured. Saxton's atlas of 1579—the first to survey the whole of England—was of little value to the traveller. The first cartographer, or topographical draughtsman, to produce maps for his specific use, was John Norden, who actually named roads on his maps, and in *An Intended Guide for English Travellers* (1625) introduced 'a new invention' of triangular distances between towns. It seems odd, on reflection, that Anglo-Saxon settlements were a thousand years old when the first correctly surveyed maps were drawn.

The measured mile of 1,760 yards, defined by Statute in 1593, appeared first in *Britannia,* by John Ogilby, Cosmographer to Charles II, in which total distances are given in four different measures: first, the direct horizontal distance (the Roman measurement); secondly, the computation; thirdly, the dimensuration, and fourthly the post office distance. For nearly a hundred years after Ogilby road books continued to give both measured and computed miles. The method of measuring is interesting. It was done by two men trundling along the road an instrument called a dimensurator, which

Berwick

Newcastle-on-
Tyne
Durham
Cockermouth
Darlington
Kendal
Lancaster York
Wentbridge
Wigan Doncaster
Conway Chester
Denbigh Newark
Caernarvon Grantham Walsingham
Lichfield Stamford Yarmouth
Coventry Huntingdon
Towcester Cambridge
Hereford Colchester
Brecknock
St Davids Gloucester Ware
Carmarthen Oxford
Marlborough LONDON
Bristol Newbury Canterbury
Basingstoke Dover
Salisbury
Chard Crewkerne
Exeter
Bodmin
Truro
St Burian

Map 11   Main roads in 'Harrison' (1577-86)

Map 12   Main roads in 'Ogilby' (1675)

was a wheel with a ten-mile length of tape round it. One man had charge of the wheel, the other marked off the distances.

John Ogilby was at pains to show bridges on his strip maps, even to giving the number of arches they had, and it may have been the importance of having such features as these properly recorded that delayed the full representation of long-distance roads. If so it stresses the revolutionary change that the arrival of wheeled transport brought about in the attitude of the man in the fields, the forerunner of the 'man in the street', towards roads. By the end of the Middle Ages most market towns could be reached from each other by alternative routes if one became impassable. These would be well known and frequently in use. When it came to providing national routes all manner of factors would come into the reckoning, not the least of which would be the weather to be expected at different times of the year. When Cary published his *Roads* he had to give a choice of six roads for the section of the Great North Road north of Boroughbridge, and he tells us that at Newark the road was so often flooded that a new turnpike was built on arches. There can be little doubt that it was circumstances such as these that delayed the appearance of roads on national atlases. After all, Norden's map of Essex, drawn in 1594, has a whole network of roads beautifully traced on it, and in 1596 a map of Kent was published with many roads shown on it.

To claim that every part of England was within a fortnight's ride of London doesn't sound very impressive to us; but it did in times when 30 miles a day was a good average to maintain over a couple of weeks. That is why Sir Robert Carey's ride to Edinburgh in 1603 continued to be discussed with wonder and incredulity for generations. The claim was that Sir Robert, a renowned place-hunter, rode a total distance of 382 miles in approximately 60 hours of riding time during the course of less than three days. He accomplished the feat in order to be the first to carry news of the Queen's death from Greenwich to the court of King James in Scotland. Riding over London Bridge at 10 o'clock on Thursday morning, he galloped up the Old North Road and reached Doncaster by nightfall. By Saturday noon he was over the Border; but during that day's ride he was thrown by his horse and kicked on the head. Although this forced him to moderate his speed he reached Edinburgh 'beblooded with great falles and bruises' just as the king was about to retire for the night, and was rewarded by being appointed one of the lords of the Bedchamber.

As in so many other fields, Elizabeth herself may well have brought about a revolutionary change in the public attitude to roads and indeed to travel in general. In one or other of her Progresses she journeyed through all the southern counties and most of those in the Midlands, and from the beginning of her reign set out to court her people—everywhere succeeding because she was so supremely in tune with the spirit of the age. The Spanish ambassador, describing a scene in 1568, wrote: 'She was received everywhere with great acclamations and signs of joy, as is customary in this country; whereat she was extremely pleased and told me so, giving me to understand how beloved she was by her subjects and how highly she esteemed this, together with the fact that they were peaceful and contented, whilst her neighbours on all sides are in such trouble. She attributes it all to God's miraculous goodness. She ordered her carriage sometimes to be taken where the crowd seemed thickest, and stood up and thanked the people'.

The reference to a carriage is interesting because she was given one by a Dutchman in 1565, so this would presumably be the one the Spanish ambassador saw in 1568. In 1572 she is recorded as having travelled to Warwick in a 'coach' constructed so that 'every part and side'could be opened to enable her subjects to have a good view of her. We do not know whether the 'carriage' of 1568 and the 'coach' of 1572 were one and the same or not; but we do know that she loved above everything else to be seen and admired, and that normally she travelled in a 'litter'. Wherever she went church bells signalled her approach so that as she passed through the villages everyone would be out to welcome her. And what occasions these Progresses were! All the great officers of state attended her, with hundreds of lesser rank, requiring in all up to 600 baggage waggons or two-wheeled carts, which must literally have meant thousands of horses. So however valuable these Progresses may have been in other respects they cannot have done the roads much good. But this may itself have highlighted their wretched condition and led to demands for their improvement.

Without doubt it was the coming on to the roads, towards the end of Elizabeth's reign, of four-wheeled waggons drawn by eight, nine, or even ten horses, carrying 60 to 70 hundredweights of grain and other produce, that brought the parishes into revolt. Few could bear the cost of bringing the roads up to the standards required to bear these heavy loads. So in 1618 a limit of five horses was imposed on four-wheeled waggons. By that time, however, James I was securely on the English throne and let it be known that there was a legal requirement for the king's highway to be maintained in a condition suitable for 'royal passage'. So that this should be fully understood, in 1621 an order was sent to the Justices of the Peace of Surrey, Essex, Middlesex, Hertford, Cambridge, and Huntingdonshire, requiring them to ensure that the roads within their jurisdiction were properly maintained before the winter set in, specifically stating, 'especially in those places where the King may have occasion to pass'.*

Similar orders were issued in succeeding years, particularly in respect of roads around Royston† and on the Newmarket road through Newport, where the house called 'Crown House' or 'Nell Gwynne's House', was formerly a posting inn patronised by the king and his courtiers. Newmarket, it must be remembered, was established as a racing centre by James I and his Scottish favourites.

This chivying by Whitehall, and the financial burden of complying with royal demands while the king was in residence at Theobalds, Cheshunt, his favourite palace, was resented by the Hertfordshire Justices, who were already overburdened by having to maintain the Old North Road as it ran through the same parishes. So in 1622 they asked that heavy four-wheeled vehicles should be entirely forbidden, and Whitehall agreed by prohibiting those with more than four wheels and loads of more than 20 cwts drawn by more than five horses. The Hertfordshire Justices were still not satisfied, so imposed further restrictions on maltsters and loaders using the road from Royston to Buntingford between All Saints' Day and May Day. To this they later added restraints on carts travelling to Ware from Buntingford.

*State Papers (Dom.) 1619-23, p.291
†For first projected turnpike (1622), See F. G. Emmison, *Bulletin of Inst. of Hist. Res.* Vol. XII, 108-112

The difference between roads with rock foundations and those that crossed swamps became most apparent with the movement of troops during the Civil War in the middle of the seventeenth century, when in order to break the defences of the kingdom the great castle strongholds that had dominated the scene since Norman times had to be attacked and destroyed. They extended from the far West to the far North, and included such key points as Corfe, Winchester, and Bristol in the West, Banbury, Dudley, and Nottingham in the Midlands, and Pontefract and Scarborough in Yorkshire. Wherever the Round-heads marched they complained that the roads impeded progress. So when they came to power they passed the 1654 Act empowering the Justices to raise revenue for the repair of roads by means of a tax on the annual value of land in the manner that had already been legalised for the repair of bridges. Expectedly, there was little enthusiasm for it in the parishes, and as it was Commonwealth legislation it lost what little respect it enjoyed at the Restoration until, in 1662, necessity compelled its re-enactment.

The second half of the seventeenth century brought a spate of eye-witness accounts of road conditions in travel diaries by Pepys, Thoresby, Evelyn, Celia Fiennes, and Sir William Dugdale, all testifying to the lamentable condition of roads, with Norfolk outstanding among the few exceptions. In 1675 John Ogilby wrote in *Britannia:* 'The roads from King's Lynn to Norwich . . . affording a very good way (much open and heathy), as indeed the whole county generally does, which makes it reported that King James once pleasantly said, he would have all Norfolk cut out into roads to supply the rest of the kingdom'.

The difference between the roads of Norfolk and the Old North Road as it passed through Hertfordshire across the bridge at Ware must have continued to gall King James as it did so many other travellers. Pepys, as a man who liked comfort, complained that it was useless for weeks at a time in wet weather. Ralph Thoresby (1658-1725) had the same complaint later. One entry in his Diary records that the rains had 'raised the washes upon the roads near Ware to the height that passengers from London that were upon the road swam, and a poor higgler was drowned, which prevented me travelling for many hours'. Towards evening, however, he and his fellow travellers were conducted 'by country folk' along tracks that skirted the flooded areas near Cheshunt, so that they were able to reach Waltham Cross safely by nightfall. Thoresby is usually factual in his evidence, but he was such a confirmed complainer that we are left wondering why he spent so much of his time travelling.

These depressing accounts of winter floods in the Lea Valley do, however, need to be balanced aginst its advantages for summer travel, which even Thoresby found pleasant and Pepys irresistible. Love of travel quickly spread with the introduction of stage coaches, which seem to have made their first appearance on English roads about 1640. At all events, in 1669 Edward Chamberlayne wrote enthusiastically in *The Present State of England;* 'There is of late such an admirable commodiousness, both for men and women of better rank, to travel from London to almost any great town of England and to almost all the villages near this great city, that the like hath not been known in the world, and that is by stage coaches, wherein one may be transported to any place sheltered from foul weather and foul ways, from endamaging one's health or body by hard jogging or over-violent motion, and this not only at a low price, as about a shilling for every five

THE POST-ROADS OF ENGLAND, 1675.

—————— DIRECT ROADS
- - - - - - - CROSS ROADS

Map 13   The Post-roads of England (1675)

miles, but with velocity and speed as that the posts in some foreign countries make not more miles a day'.

Accounts of conditions in different parts of England continued to be conflicting until well into the eighteenth century. The Cotswold through-roads, which kept to the ridge-ways, were good. The wealthy wool merchants contributed to their maintenance as they did to the maintenance and rebuilding of churches. Thomas Deloney, writing at the beginning of the seventeenth century, when most merchants sent their goods by pack-horse, described how the cloth wains of Cole of Reading held up a Royal Progress so long that the courtiers began to wonder if 'Old Cole had got a commission for all the carts in the country to carry his cloth'. South of London the sharpest contrasts in road conditions were in Kent and Sussex. The Dover road was always well maintained; but elsewhere the heavy loads of iron from the furnaces put the roads out of use for long periods until a Statute of Elizabeth I required iron-masters carrying loads for one mile or more on any highway between 12 October and 1 May to carry a cartload of cinders, gravel, stone, sand, or chalk for the repair of the roads they passed along.

In view of the complaints that continued to be made about the Sussex roads it is doubtful whether this measure was ever as effective as it was intended to be. There were times when judges on circuit would only attend summer assizes at Horsham, and as late as 1690 one judge, Spencer Cowper, wrote to his wife that Sussex roads were 'bad and ruinous beyond imagination. I vow 'tis melancholy consideration that mankind will inhabit such a heap of dirt for a poor livelihood. The County is a sink of about fourteen miles broad, which receives all the water that falls from two long ranges of hills on both sides of it'. Throughout most of the eighteenth century judges continued to ride their circuits wrapped in thick riding cloaks with jackboots up to their hips. They certainly needed them when they rode to Horsham, as we know from a petition from the people of that town presented to Parliament as late as 1750, praying 'for a passable carriage road to London, the road by Coldharbour and Dorking, which had superseded the excellent Roman road, being accessible only on horseback'. One of the worst accounts of a coach journey in Sussex is that of a visit made in 1703 by Prince George of Denmark to Pet-worth House to meet Charles III of Spain there. The last nine miles of the journey took six hours. No wonder Dr Burton gravely expressed the personal opinion that all the animals in Sussex, including the human, had long legs as the result of the continuous pulling of them out of the mud as they walked.

Progress was even slower in the West of England, where Tom Pierce and his cronies at Widecombe Fair had too much confidence in the sure-footed Dartmoor ponies to risk their lives in any alternative form of transport. William Marshall in his *Early Tours* (1796) wrote: 'Less than half a century ago they [the lanes] were mere gullies, worn by torrents in the rocks, which appeared in steps or staircases, with fragments lying loose in the indentures. Speaking with little if any latitude, there was not then a wheel carriage in the district, nor, fortunately for the necks of travellers, any horses but those which were native to the country'. As these Devon lanes could only have been widened at prohibitive expense to carry coaches, the introduction of any form of wheeled vehicle into the county was exceptionally late. When coaches did eventually arrive new roads were made for them, most of them dating from the first decade of the nineteenth cen-

KEY
Roman Road ·················
Ogilby's Road --------
Modern Trunk Road ———

Map 14   The Great North Road

tury. They can be recognised by the way they bypass the old villages. There are none, for example, on the road from Exeter to Barnstaple, and they are only found on the old section of the road from Exeter to Okehampton.

As late as 1889, Baring-Gould in *Old Country Life* tells us that he employed a coachman who had been with his family for 75 years and was able to remember how the roads were made before McAdam's system was introduced. The groundwork was of large stones. This was topped with small stones gathered from the fields, which were ground down by the carts and waggons that passed over them. When asked how fragile goods could be carried along such roads without breaking, the old coachman explained that they were carried by pack-horse and showed where the old packhorse trails ran through the woods and alongside the modernised roads.

'"Ah, sir!" said my old coachman, "them was jolly times. The packmen used to travel in a lot together, and when they put up at an inn for the night, there was fun—not but what they was a bit rough-like .... Packmen at times carried a lot o' money about with them, and it did happen now and then that lonely packmen were robbed and murdered".' He could remember a time when Baring-Gould's grandfather, who was both squire and parson, was the only man in the parish to own a waggon or any other conveyance. Everyone else travelled on horseback and brought in crops on sledges.

This bypassing of villages in Devon is in contrast to what happened along the Great North Road. There long and bitter legal battles were fought to keep the roads routed through the villages so that the traders and innkeepers could continue to enjoy the advantages derived from travellers. Many of these, especially the innkeepers, were men of substance. Defoe tells us how Doncaster owed its prosperity in his day to the determination of its inhabitants to have it firmly astride the main road. They were led by the mayor, who was also the landlord of the post-house, postmaster, owner of a good stable and in all respects lived in the style of a gentleman, with his own pack of hounds.

But with London expanding the main problems continued to be in connection with the roads across claylands to the north, through which most of the coaches had to plough their way at the start of their journeys. John Bunyan's 'Slough of Despond' was a fair description of one of the worst stretches—an especially vicious bog on the London road near Bedford, of which he wrote: 'It was not the pleasure of the king that this should be so bad . . . to my knowledge there have been swallowed up at least twenty thousand cart loads . . . the best materials to make good ground of the place'. The only effective way of dealing with such places before modern road-making methods were introduced was to lay logs across them to form a corduroy road. Remains of such roads are constantly being dug up where deep excavations are required for motorways. On the whole, however, local feeling was passive. There was a cherished saw: 'There is good land where there is foul way' and it was usually true. Its northern version was 'Where there's muck there's money'.

So it came about that it was on the Old North Road that the first Turnpike was installed under the provisions of the Act of 1663 'for the repairing of highways within the counties of Hertford, Cambridge, and Huntingdon'. By the time the Act was passed the constant winter flooding of the road in the neighbourhood of Ware had become further aggravated by the large quantities of barley and malt taken into the town to be carried by water to London. The parish of Standon, between Wadesmill and Bunting-ford, was the most frequently presented for grievances attributed to this cause. With the object of making funds available for radical road improvements the Hertfordshire Justices were enabled under the Act to levy tolls at Wadesmill, near Ware, the Cambridgeshire Justices at Caxton, and the Huntingdonshire Justices at Stilton. When passed, the Act was regarded as a temporary measure to deal with an emergency situation and a term of 11 years was specified for its operation. In 1665, however, this had to be extended to 21 years. In fact, the only toll gate to be established for the collection of tolls was one at Wadesmill. One was set-up at Caxton; but it was so easily bypassed that it failed to collect the expected revenue, and the one at Stilton met with so much local opposition that it was never started. In the light of this experience the next Turnpike Act did not appear on the Statute Book until 30 years later.

The Act that came into operation in the last decade of the century not only granted power to collect tolls on roads as far apart as the one from Harwich to London and the one from Birdlip to Gloucester, but authorised the setting up of barriers to prevent travellers using them without paying. This was an important new concession. There had been no reference to barriers in the 1663 Act. Despite this, the objects of these first Acts were not achieved. By the turn of the century most of the toll gates were either broken down or abandoned and the roads between them were again being described as 'dangerous and impassable'.

CHAPTER SEVEN

Coach Roads

———◆◆◆———

THE TURNPIKE system was unpopular from start to finish; but was accepted finally because it appeared to be a necessary evil. Macaulay, describing the process of acceptance, said that 'by slow degrees reason triumphed over prejudice; and our island is now crossed by nearly thirty thousand miles of turnpike road'. In fact, reason triumphing over prejudice had very little to do with the process, although it must be admitted that at the end of the eighteenth century the system did appear to be working. In nothing is this attitude of resistance to turnpikes and their keepers more graphically expressed than in *Pickwick Papers,* where Tony Weller, turning to Mr Pickwick says:

"Wery queer life is a pike-keeper's, sir".

"A what?" said Mr. Pickwick. . . .

"The old 'un means a turnpike keeper, gen'lm'n," observed Mr. Samuel Weller, in explanation.

"Oh," said Mr. Pickwick, "I see. Yes; very curious life—very uncomfortable".

"They're all on 'em men as has met vith some disappointment in life . . . consequence of vich they retires from the world, and shuts themselves up in pikes; partly vith the view of being solitary, and partly to rewenge themselves on mankind by takin' tolls. . . . If they was gen'lm'n, you'd call 'em misanthropes, but as it is, they only turns to pike-keepin'".

The point to this conversation is that it shows that the 'curious' attitude, to use Mr Pickwick's word, that had persisted through 300 years of regarding road surveyors as men to be ostracised had been transferred to pike-keepers. All through the eighteenth century toll-gates were being either broken or burnt, which might be thought odd since the levying of tolls for the use of repairing roads was the same in principle as the levying of pontage for the repair of bridges. In 1732 a riotous armed mob marched into Hereford threatening not only to destroy the turnpikes but to murder the pikemen and the trustees who employed them. Lancashire men fought long against their introduction. But there the conflict was between the sporting landed gentry, many of whom were members of long-established Roman Catholic families, and the new industrialists of the early years of the Industrial Revolution. Why, asked the gentry, should their woodlands be felled, their game scared away, and their parks disfigured for the convenience of 'the dingy denizens of Manchester, or the purse-proud merchants of Liverpool? Miry roads were a price they were willing to pay for the conservation of Merry England, the survival of the fox in his earth, the bittern by his pool, and the wild fowl on the marshes of the Fylde.

Consequently Arthur Young, writing in 1770 said that he could not find 'in the whole range of language terms sufficiently expressive to describe' the 'infernal road' from Wigan to Preston.

The reason why this particular stretch of road remained bad so long was that London carriers travelling north found it more profitable to discharge their cargo at Wigan and load up with coal for the return journey instead of continuing to Preston. But the whole of the North lagged behind the South in road-making during the eighteenth century. The first turnpikes in Derbyshire were set up about 1720; but when roads were made from Manchester to such places as Buxton and Chapel-en-le-Frith, most of them ended when they reached the limestone plateau. Roderick Random, travelling from Glasgow to London in 1739 found 'no such convenience as a wagon' in the northern counties, and 'set out with the carriers who transport goods from one place to another on horseback'. He reached Newcastle-upon-Tyne 'sitting upon a pack-saddle between two baskets'. Seventy years later, when Sydney Smith arrived at his new parish of Foston-le-Clay in the Yorkshire Wolds in a four-wheeled carriage, the whole village turned out to see it, and when a few years later again a coach was seen approaching the village the parish clerk, the sexton, and the vicar's churchwarden all rushed to tell the parson.

Conditions changed rapidly in the second half of the eighteenth century over most of the country. Three hundred and eighty-nine Trusts were established during the 22 years 1751-1772. There was even a popular demand for them in the prosperous wool towns of Frome, Trowbridge, and the West Midlands. When the Burslem potters, led by Josiah Wedgwood, petitioned Parliament in 1763 for a turnpike road that would bypass Newcastle-under-Lyme the people of Newcastle counter-petitioned for one that did not go 'only through small villages, so that the same seems solely calculated to serve the interests of a few private persons'. The opponents of turnpikes, however, described this new movement in their favour as 'turnpike mania'. And no-one was oblivious to the fact that as the number of toll-gates increased so did the number of tolls to be paid. To this irritation was added the frustration of long delays at night, when, as Dickens found, there was 'the stopping at the turnpike where the man was gone to bed, and knocking at the door until he answered with a smothered shout from under the bedclothes in the little room above, where the faint light was burning, and presently came down, night-capped and shivering, to throw the gate wide open, and wish all the waggons off the road except by day'.*

No wonder Hazy in *Facey Romford* 'never disturbed a pikeman, if he could help it'.

This reluctant acceptance found Parliamentary expression in 1773 when a General Turnpike Act was passed, drawing attention to the impossibility of maintaining through-routes while local variations continued, and opening up the way for national economic expansion by extending provisions for money to be raised by taxation for the repair of roads. It had finally dawned on the law-makers that instead of trying to adapt traffic to the roads the roads must be adapted to traffic.

Industrial factors were not the only considerations in promoting this change of attitude. If they had been, the landed interests might still have stood out against it. It

*The Old Curiosity Shop, chap. XLVI

17 Turnpike toll charge board, Stroud

18 Toll-gate, St Clement's, Oxford

cannot have been without significance that just as the Civil War in the middle of the seventeenth century had alerted Parliament to the inadequacy of the national road system, the 1745 Rebellion had alerted it again and this time more effectively. The shocking condition of the highway between Carlisle and General Wade's headquarters at Newcastle-upon-Tyne was the sole and fatal reason for his failure to reach the one from the other in time. It was to remedy this defence weakness that his army constructed the road—still called the Military Road—which follows the line of the Roman Wall for 30 miles, using much of its material for the purpose.

By that time the main roads between London and Chester, Exeter, and York were in good repair. The journeys along all three could be made by coach in four days so long as 40 horses could be counted upon to be in readiness for changes along the routes. In a book entitled *Old Roads and New Roads,* published in 1852, W. B. Donne says: 'We have before us an announcement . . . dated in the year 1751. It sets forth that, God willing, the new Expedition coach will leave the 'Maid's Head', Norwich, on Wednesday or Thursday morning, at seven o'clock, and arrive at the 'Boar' in Aldgate on the Friday or Saturday, "as shall seem good" to the majority of the passengers. It appears from the appellation of the vehicle "the New Expedition", that such a rate of journeying was considered to be an advance in speed, and an innovation worthy of general notice and patronage. Fifty years before the same journey had occupied a week; and in 1664 Christopher Milton, the poet's brother and afterwards one of James II's Justices, had taken eight-and-forty hours to go from the 'Belle Sauvage' to Ipswich'.

In considering these speeds it has to be borne in mind that throughout the eighteenth century coaches continued to be drawn by horses bred for farm work. Only heavily built horses could have drawn even the lighter coaches at that time. It may be recalled that when Jane Austen's family removed from Deane to Steventon in 1771 the road was a mere cart track, so Mrs Austen travelled the short distance lying on a feather bed placed on soft pieces of furniture in the waggon carrying the family's household goods.

The really revolutionary date in the history of roads is 1784, when John Palmer, a theatre proprietor of Bath, conceived the idea of sending mails by coach. Before that date they had been carried by post-boys. During the later years of the century this postal service so transformed the coaching trade that 80 mail coaches, each drawn by four horses, left London every evening, and each had either four or six passengers inside whose fares, it was claimed, covered the cost of carrying the mail. Each coach had a guard armed with a blunderbuss. The praises of these new coaches were sung as coaches had never before had their praises sung and seldom since until Washington Irving caught the

19 Birmingham Tally-ho! Coaches (from a painting by James Pollard, engraved by C. Bentley)

coaching spirit in the single sentence: 'A stage coach carries animation always with it, and puts the world in motion as it whirls along'.

Under risk of incurring a penalty of 40 shillings the pikemen were required to have the gates open for the mail coaches to pass through at speed, and to enliven their approach, which was the most exciting event in the day for the villages and small towns, the guard would sound a horn or a key-bugle on which he might play the popular airs of the day with a vigour that like John Peel's hunting horn might have awakened the dead. But as the mails travelled free of tolls the requests of the Postmaster General for better roads were not always sympathetically received.

Mail coaches will always be associated in the popular mind with highwaymen, because although footpads were already on the roads before the stage coaches arrived, their nefarious way of life had become extremely lucrative now they were mounted and could achieve a quick get-away. Every highway had its 'black-spots' for hold-ups. Epping Forest, Hampstead Heath, and Hounslow Heath were the most notorious in the Home Counties, with Dick Turpin in Epping Forest and James Maclaine, the son of a Presbyterian minister, on Hounslow Heath. Maclaine was one of the 'gentlemen highwaymen', who followed in the tradition of Claude Duval, a Frenchman who came to England in the service of the Duke of Richmond and was so popular with the fair sex that when he was awaiting execution in 1670, so many ladies of exalted rank pleaded for his life that only the judge's threat that he would resign if Duval didn't hang prevented his being

20 The Highgate Road, c. 1830 (from a painting by James Pollard, engraved by G. Hunt)

pardoned. One story told of him was that after robbing a traveller of £400 he returned £300 on the victim's wife consenting to dance with him.

On Duval's tombstone in Covent Garden churchyard was inscribed the epitaph:

> *Here lies Du Val. Reader, if male thou art,*
> *Look to thy purse; if female to thy heart.*
> *Much havoc he has made of both; for all*
> *Men he made stand, and women he made fall.*
> *The second conqueror of the Norman race,*
> *Knights to his arms did yield and Ladies to his face.*
> *Old Tyburn's Glory, England's illustrious thief,*
> *Du Val, the ladies' joy, Du Val, the ladies' grief.*

Most of the eighteenth-century highwaymen had idiosyncracies that have appealed to writers of romantic fiction far more than they can have commended them to their victims. Captain James Hind, who once held up Oliver Cromwell's coach near Hunting-don, made much of his habit of returning a small token of his loot for the victim's 'luck'. No doubt he believed that this would be put forward in mitigation if he were caught. It failed. He was hanged, drawn and quartered at Worcester.

Swift wrote of one of these practical jokers, Tom Clinch, that on his way to be hanged at Tyburn,

> *He stopt at 'The Bowl' for a bottle of sack*
> *And promised to pay for it when he came back.*

On the whole the acquittals of highwaymen are more curious than their convictions. One of the most remarkable was at Hertford Assizes in 1758 in a case in which the principal witness against a highwayman named Page was the fourth Earl Ferrers. The evidence was that when accosted by Page the earl had drawn out a pistol, but his hand had trembled so much that he had been unable to fire it and the highwayman had taken it from him. Page again escaped death at the trial by submitting that since the earl had been excommunicated he was not competent to give evidence. This was accepted by the judge and he was acquitted.

Horace Walpole gave an account of this trial in his *Letters,* where he also tells the story of how Lady Browne and he were stopped by a black figure on horseback demand-ing their purses and watches. Lady Browne handed over her purse and was about to hand over her watch when he said: 'I am much obliged to you. I wish you good night', doffed his hat and rode away. When Horace Walpole tried to comfort her by pointing out that the highwayman had been less fierce than might have been expected she replied: 'But I am in terror lest he should return, for I have given him a purse with only bad money in it that I carry on purpose'.

One of several odd ways in which the scales of justice were weighted in favour of the criminal—and we still have a few—was that if a man fell a victim to a highwayman when travelling on the sabbath he had no redress in law. Most of these odd quirks were hang-

21 Dick Turpin holding up the York stage-coach

overs from earlier and more godfearing days, which also gave rise to a spate of superstitions about lonely stretches of the highway, and in particular about cross-roads, which
were often places of execution or where suicides were buried. These also were derived
from a pious wish to offer the soul of the departed to the mercy of God, since by ancient
custom crosses had been erected at cross roads. Many of these corners came to be
regarded as haunted, and when accidents occurred at them supernatural agencies were
suspected.

In the hope of preventing those buried at cross roads from rising to do further evil,
stakes were often driven through their hearts. In 1823 this came to an end by the passing
of an Act forbidding such burials and requiring a piece of unconsecrated ground to be set
aside in all cemeteries for the burial of unhallowed corpses. The roadside burial of one
such unhallowed corpse is marked by 'Clibbon's Post' near Queen Hoo Hall, one mile
north-west of Bramfield in Hertfordshire, where Walter Clibbon, or Clibborn, a
notorious murderer, was buried with a stake driven through his heart after being shot
dead himself on 28 December 1782. The story goes that Clibbon made a pretence of
earning an honest living as a pieman in Hertford market so that he could discover which
farmers were likely to return home with most money on them. Then, assisted by his wife
and sons he would choose a suitable place to waylay and rob them. His victim on the
night of the first market after Christmas 1782 was a farmer named Benjamin Whittenbury, who was attacked just before safely reaching his home. The tables were turned,

however, when Whittenbury's cries for help were heard by his family and servants, one of whom ran with a gun to his master's aid. Clibbon, although apparently cornered, was not deterred. Instead of taking flight he knocked Whittenbury down and pulled out a clasp knife to stab him.

'Shoot, Shock, or I'm a dead man' Whittenbury shouted. Shock obeyed and Clibbon was killed.

Now, more happily, we associate cross roads with wooden signposts, which seem to date from the sixteenth century. There was certainly a signpost in Kent in 1598, and Celia Fiennes, writing in 1695, found them general at cross roads in Lancashire. Modern signposts developed from the 'handing-posts' erected on their estates by landowners in the eighteenth century. They took their name from the custom of shaping the ends of the arms into 'hands' pointing in the required direction like policemen on point duty. Probably the earliest surviving signpost is 'Cross Hands' near the crest of Broadway Hill in the Cotswolds, which has iron arms pointing respectively towards Warwick, Oxford, Gloucester, and Worcester. It was erected in 1669 by a member of the Izod family of Chipping Campden. Local tradition maintains that the iron spike at the top was used to impale sheep-stealers. Whether it was actually used for that purpose may be doubted; but it would be an impressive warning of what might be expected.

Several Cotswold handposts have been interestingly recorded in *The Minor Pleasures of Cotswold* by Edith Brill and Peter Turner—among them a stone pillar with hands

22 The Plymouth Fly, from a drawing by Thomas Rowlandson

projecting from it, called Teddington Hands, which stands at the junction of the road from Evesham with the A438, and bears the inscription:

Edward Attwood of the Vine Tree
At the first time erected me
And freely he did this bestow
Strange travellers the way to show.

Many Cotswold woolmen, who during their lives did so much for the repair of churches, left money in their wills for the repair of roads. In fact the whole subject of bequests for roads could make an interesting subject for local history societies.

Signposts cannot have been universal in the seventeenth century, or a traveller as experienced as Pepys, travelling with his wife in his own coach, would not have been lost twice within an hour, and on the second occasion so narrowly have escaped having to pass a comfortless night on Salisbury Plain. Nor would Ralph Thoresby, who lived at Leeds, have actually lost his way between Doncaster and York.

Turnpike Trusts brought milestones back to roads that had been without them since the Romans left and the Saxons broke them up. The first came in 1663, the year of the first Turnpike Act, to mark distances along the Dover road. The Great North Road got them in 1708; but what W. G. Hoskins calls 'the first true milestone' was the 1727 stone, still to be seen at Trumpington, one of a series set up between Barkway and Cambridge by the Master and Fellows of Trinity Hall, who appear to have assumed responsibility for this road in accordance with the arrangement referred to in the last chapter.* The remade section of this highway was at one time known as 'The Recorder's Road', in commemoration of the interest taken in getting it improved by Samuel Henry Pont, Recorder of Cambridge and Fellow of Trinity Hall—largely, no doubt, for his own benefit in riding down from London.

As stone was not everywhere available, many Trusts could only provide wooden posts. Those set up by the Epping and Ongar Turnpike Trust in 1787 were of oak, with two faces set at an angle, each with Epping on one side and the next important town on the other. Many of these early milestones served the dual purpose of milestone and mounting-block. In some districts they were called upping-stones. We find them across Dunsmore in Warwickshire, and mounting-steps are cut into the stone at Bulls Cross on the road from Stroud to Cheltenham. Again, where stone was not at hand they were in the form of wooden steps. Most of these have rotted away; but the one outside Epping Old Church is kept in good repair although no-one uses it now. At Wingfield Church in Suffolk there is a mounting-stone let into the churchyard wall, which is reached by climbing three steps, and mounting-blocks are let into other churchyard walls in the eastern counties, where stone is scarce. There is one to be seen at Bradwell-on-Sea in Essex. In the iron-producing districts of the Midlands nineteenth-century cast-iron milestones are still common, especially on the main roads in Staffordshire and Derbyshire—notably along the road from Leek to Newcastle-under-Lyme, Buxton, and Ashbourne. Incidentally, two fine cast-iron bridges, the Chetwynd Bridge, near Alrewas, and

23 Wilton Bridge Milestone and Sundial, Wiltshire   See page 88

the High Bridge over the Trent near Ridwares were erected by the Coalbrookdale Company.

Gradually the expansion of industry and the better conditions of work to be found in the towns led to the depopulation of the countryside, and a new social conflict broke out between the gentry and those who saw that if the rapidly increasing population was to be fed, agriculture would have to be organised on industrial lines, and vast areas of unused land brought into production. To accomplish this, waste land must be enclosed and more intensive methods of cultivation encouraged. In the event these enclosures were to revolutionise the rural landscape as drastically as mechanisation was later to revolutionise the urban. Marshes were drained, commons enclosed, scrub cleared and woodlands felled. It is not difficult to imagine the protests. They are repeated in every generation, and nowhere more typically than in John Byng's lament on the effect of the improvement of road transport written in 1781: 'I wish with all my heart that half the turnpike roads in the kingdom were plough'd up, which have imported London manners, and depopulated the country. I meet milkmaids on the road, with the dress and looks of Strand misses; and must think that every line of Goldsmith's *Deserted Village* contains melancholy truths'.

The transformation of the countryside was accomplished by three means: Acts of Parliament permitting enclosures, local consent, and orders by Commissioners empowered to make enclosure awards. As private enclosure Acts were costly, the awards made by the Commissioners were the most far-reaching in their effect on roads, particularly along the coast. Under them the landscape was carved up into regular shapes and patterns, encased in equally regularly shaped roads. Where the old roads had originally run round ponds and large trees, following for the most part ancient cattle trails, the new ones were like the lines on a chequer board. They can best be seen across the broad Midland belt that became the workshop of England, but which still has attractive, if overplanned countryside between its towns.

In this replanning the obvious first-step was to get the byways straightened and shortened to take the new traffic; but when this was attempted it was found that many apparently irrational lines could not be straightened because they defined boundaries. Although it was pointed out that many of these boundary ways had begun as baulks between ploughed furlongs that were no longer there, it was held that as boundaries they had acquired inalienable rights with the authority of land charters supporting them. However, when the question of whether something could be done to annul those rights, to which the answer was invariably 'No', was amended to how it could be done, the lawyers, as usual, found a way, and the Commissioners were allowed to negotiate suitable settlements with the landowners that gave them what they wanted without prolonged litigation. The affluence that followed the Napoleonic wars provided the money.

So within the space of a couple of generations vast areas of the Midlands acquired a new look, which provided for long-distance coaches to pass through populous counties speedily and safely, and brought the scores of new towns in this broadest part of England within reach of through-routes north and south, giving the region great advantages for expanding trade.

24 Milestone on Alconbury Hill, Huntingdonshire

25, 26 Milestone at Crows-an-Wra, West Penwith, Cornwall

TO
PENZANCE
5½
MILES.

TO
LANDSEND
4½
MILES.

But not all the new roads were made by competent engineers. Every motorist must have had the experience of pressing his foot on the accelerator pedal on seeing a straight stretch of road in front of him, then almost immediately having to brake because the apparently well-made straight road turned out to be a switch-back. If the fields on either side of the road are of the regular shapes just described, he would probably find on enquiry at the local Record Office that the deceptive road dated from the enclosure awards, and the reason for the switch-back effect was that it had been constructed across ridges of ploughed land which had not been adequately drained and levelled along the passage of the road. In short, he had been jolted because he had driven over ancient ridges. In the evening light these ridges can often be seen casting shadows across the grass in fields bordering such roads.

The Commissioners were tidy-minded people. They grouped their newly fenced fields compactly round newly built farm houses, so many of which in this part of England are Georgian. When we compare the hedgerows along these Commissioners' roads with those in early enclosed counties like Suffolk, Essex, Kent and Devon, we see how much more history there is to read into the old hedges. Nevertheless, the planters of the new hedges did follow traditional methods. It was at this time that the art of laying quick hedges became universal. Cobbett admired them greatly. Writing in 1822 to record a ride from Royston to Huntingdon he says: 'The fields on the left seem to have been enclosed by Act of Parliament; and they certainly are the most beautiful fields that I ever saw . . . divided by quickset hedges, exceedingly well planted and raised'.

Ditches are another indication of the age of a road. Between the extremes of the Fenland dykes and the shallow quick-flowing gullies of the moorland counties there are grades of depth and shape that tell us much, especially about the soil. In regions of intensive agriculture ditches dominate, in parkland hedgerows neatly trimmed were favoured by eighteenth-century improvers. Then there are tell-tale roadside features like the small quarries that border roads in hill country, now so often used as sheltered places to draw off the road for a picnic. They were provided for the repair of roads before the age of Telford and McAdam, just as in the South roadside ponds are frequently the result of gravel diggings for the same purpose.

The remnants of pre-enclosure lanes in the Midlands can often be recognised near villages that were bypassed during the period as farmways, with straggling remains of old hedgerows that have become sanctuaries for wild flowers and birds in spring, when the old ditches are full of primroses, and are bountiful with blackberries in autumn.

An inevitable result of so many Turnpike Trusts coming into operation at once was a spate of articles theorising about methods of road construction, largely inspired by the need to find the cheapest method possible, simply because most of the Trusts were too poor to afford orthodox methods. The *Annual Register* for 1775 recorded that an experiment tried on the Ipswich road had 'answered beyond expectation', which begs the question of 'Whose expectation?' The only original feature of this experiment was that instead of the raised *agger* of the Roman road, a convex method was introduced that was so extreme that it produced the effect of a line of sunken barrels. The object was to achieve maximum drainage; but as the road was surfaced with rough stones that were scattered to the sides every time a heavy vehicle passed along it a team of men had to be employed to throw them back. Still more serious was the danger of coaches overturning on meeting one coming in the opposite direction, to say nothing of the strain put on the fetlock joints of the horses.

Incredible as it may now appear, the reverse method was tried elsewhere of providing for water to run along the roadway instead of being drained off it in the belief that as the water would wash away the soft parts of the road a firm carriageway would eventually be achieved. This method was promulgated by a certain gentleman named Robert Phillips in a work published in 1737 entitled *A Dissertation concerning the Present State of the High Roads of England,* in which it was argued that if the roads were lower than the bordering land instead of higher, the water would drain naturally into the land. In support of this extraordinary argument he pointed out that the beds of rivers were hard and smooth as the result of the action of the water that flowed over them. This water method was tried with chaotic results at Ware in Hertfordshire.

In course of time three men turned up with the right answers, although by no means agreeing with each other. The first was John Metcalf—Blind Jack of Knaresborough— who had been musician, soldier, pedlar, fish-dealer, horse-dealer and common carrier before running his own stage-waggon and deciding that something should be done about those accursed Yorkshire roads. Before he died in 1810 he had constructed 200 miles of good roadway, starting with three miles between Harrogate and Boroughbridge in his native parts. His method was completely orthodox: namely, to lay a firm foundation, then give it a moderately curved surface to carry off the rainwater. The other two, Thomas Telford and John Loudon McAdam, were almost exact contemporaries. Telford lived from 1757 to 1834, McAdam from 1756 to 1836. Like John Metcalf they were men of superhuman drive and character. What is most remarkable in view of their being contemporaries is that they worked throughout their lives on diametrically opposed principles—principles as opposed as the convex and concave principles that had failed so lamentably before them. The explanation of the success of both these extra-ordinary characters is that Telford, the 'safe' man, had the support of the Postmaster-General, with whom cost was not a prime consideration, while McAdam, the innovator, had the support of the Office of Works because his methods were so much cheaper than Telford's. In days when cars were not as powerful as they are now, it used to be said that you could tell whether you were on a Telford or a McAdam road by the number of times you had to change gear; but this was rather unfairly critical of McAdam because Telford got the best routes to work on.

Thomas Telford was the son of a Dumfriesshire shepherd, but was born and learned his trade in Eskdale as a journeyman mason building bridges across the fast-flowing streams of the Lake District and later of Scotland. This meant that he knew both the strength of stone and the strength of water, and had a Northerner's respect for both. His method was to lay a six-inch layer of broken stones on a foundation of large stones, and surface with gravel, taking care that the stones were properly pitched and cambered for drainage: the method that had been tried and tested for more than a thousand years and had never failed. How mad, then, must McAdam have appeared to the orthodox road engineers of the day when he reversed the process and relied, not on the strength of the foundation but on the strength of the surfacing. When he claimed success, his critics

Map 15   Coach roads in 'Paterson' (1771)

argued that all he had done was repair and resurface roads that were already well founded; but they were confounded when he made a good road across a peat bog between Wedmore and Glastonbury, and another between Bridgwater and Cross in Somerset.

McAdam did not in fact invent the method associated with his name. It had been used for years in Switzerland, Sweden, and other countries, and had been anticipated in England by Gilbert Stone of Axbridge. It was the volume of his work that caused his name to give a new word to the English language. The Turnpike Trusts were quickly queueing up for his services and he never disappointed one of them. As 'Capability' Brown got his reputation by inspiring potential clients with the 'capabilities' of their estates for landscaping, McAdam gave each Trust he interviewed the feeling that their particular stretch of road was the one he had been looking for all his life and couldn't fail to be an enormous success when given his special surfacing. In course of time he was in charge of so many new roads that he employed a staff of 300 sub-surveyors, and by the end of his life he had revolutionised the whole concept of road-making.

Whether it is actually a pen portrait of McAdam himself or of one of his sub-surveyors may not be entirely clear; but I like to think we have the man to the life in Mary Russell Mitford's *Our Village,* when she writes: 'our surveyor', although bringing chaos to the village, is 'so civil and good-humoured, has such a bustling and happy self-importance, such an honest earnestness in his vocation (which is gratuitous, by-the-bye), and such an intense conviction that the state of the turnpike road between B. and K. is the principal affair of his life, that I would not undeceive him for the world. How often have I seen him on a cold winter morning, with a face all frost and business, great-coated up to the eyes, driving from post to post, from one gang of labourers to another, praising, scolding, ordering, cheated, laughed at, and liked by them all!'

The master had arrived. Daniel Paterson's *New and Accurate Description of all the Direct and Principal Cross-Roads in Great Britain,* which had superseded Ogilby's *Britannia* in 1771, was in its eighteenth edition in 1829, and continued to be the standard work on roads until the Ordnance Survey maps began to appear in 1890. There was no successor to McAdam in the history of the turnpikes. But his reign was brief. Within ten years of the introduction of the main line railways most of the Turnpike Trusts were bankrupt, and it would have been useless for the Government to take them over and reorganise them. Their debts were too heavy. They could only be left to die natural deaths, which they did more quickly than could have been believed possible when McAdam was in his prime. There were 854 of them in 1871, only two in 1890, and the last toll-gates—those on the Holyhead Road in Anglesey—went out of business in 1895.

Looking back on the system from the privileged position of the twentieth century, we may feel that in the circumstances of the eighteenth there was a good deal to commend it. It was a reasonable compromise between the view that roads were parish responsibilities, primarily for the use of the local community, and the view that they were for the free passage of all the king's subjects who cared to use them. When wheeled transport came into universal use it was clearly unfair that the parishes should be required to bear the entire cost of maintaining highways being increasingly used by rich merchants who contributed nothing to their upkeep. The turnpike system provided for everyone to contribute to the maintenance of roads in proportion to the use they made of them.

The real weakness of the system was that it relied on private enterprise for what must eventually become a national responsibility, which meant that it worked so unevenly that it satisfied neither those who saw it as an abandonment of the principle of free passage along the highway nor those who resented paying for the use of their own roads. In practice it turned out to have the additional built-in weakness that the tolls collected in rural areas, where the worst roads were found, could never reach anything approaching the amounts required to achieve the standard expected for coach travel.

With the coming of the railways the coaches also vanished, and every Christmas we are reminded that they were as popular as the turnpikes were unpopular. In contrast to Tony Weller's opinion of pikemen we have Tony himself, the immortal representative of all his kind, with their red faces under broad-brimmed hats, their John Bull bodies resplendantly buttoned up in capacious great-coats—called Benjamins—under layers of cape, their legs encased in jockey boots. They are as English as Pickwick himself.

All we have left to remind us of those days, apart from the inns to be recalled in the next chapter, are a few toll houses, and those are rapidly disappearing under road-widening schemes because they were always built close to the edge of the roadway.

27 Toll-gate at bridge over the Enborne, Berkshire

28 *Toll-gate, New Cross, Kent*

Although different Trusts had their own style, and some houses, like the one outside
Newbury, were like estate lodges, all were sufficiently conventional to be recognised for
what they were. A few were round, most were hexagonal or square, with an occasional
one half-octagonal, which gives us the clue to the principle behind their designs, which
was to provide windows facing every direction from which a coach might come. In view
of the number that would be required quickly in the late eighteenth century we may
wonder whether at the height of the turnpike era there were travelling masons—freemasons
—touring the country building them, in the way Telford and others toured the Lake
District building bridges. In another twenty or thirty years' time we shall only have place-
names to remind us where they stood. Fortunately there are several on the Great North
Road; but the only toll-house left on that road now is Barnsdale Bar, where the
Pontefract road leaves the main road.

CHAPTER EIGHT

Coaching Inns

As THERE ARE more than a hundred inns in Dickens, and 22 in *Pickwick* alone, it is not surprising that we can no more think of *Pickwick* without thinking of coaching inns than we can think of Dickens without thinking of *Pickwick.* The Golden Age of the coaching inn began in the 1820s and ended in the 1840s. *Pickwick Papers,* completed in 1837, caught the age at its zenith, when the bustle of inn yards was so great that Cobbett, whose *Rural Rides* was published in 1830, exclaimed that next to a fox hunt the arrival of a stage coach was the most exciting event to be seen anywhere in England. Dickens had watched both arrivals and departures while working so miserably at Warren's Blacking Factory near Charing Cross, at the time when only a stone's throw away, on the present site of Nelson's Column, stood the 'Golden Cross' inn from which the Pickwickians set out for Rochester.

Adding to the routine excitement of getting the horses harnessed and the passengers packed into the coaches, pedlars and mountebanks thronged the inn yards with wares and nostrums which, according to Surtees, might include a tame squirrel or a bullfinch that could whistle 'God Save the King' or 'The White Cockade' being offered in exchange for an old coat. No other writers understood the coaching trade better than Dickens and Surtees. Both were at their best in a world that combined low cunning with breezy humanity, and were themselves larger than life in merriment. Either could have gleefully recorded the senior Weller's shrewd comment that 'coaches is like guns—they requires to be loaded with werry great care, afore they go off'.

Loading was only one of the skills that had to be acquired by the Tony Wellers if their coaches were to be safely balanced. The 'wheelers', as the horses attached to the coaches were called, had to be carefully paired for equal stride if the passengers were not to be jolted. The 'leaders' in front of them had no effect on balance, so 'wheelers' and 'leaders' were seldom interchangeable. Before brakes were fitted, the safety of a coach in descending a hill depended entirely on the ability of the 'wheelers' to hold it on the bends even when the wheels were 'tied', as they would be down Porlock; and entirely when they were not, down such long descents as Broadway Hill in the Cotswolds. No wonder passengers were so ready to get out and walk.

Before the mails brought prosperity to the coaching business, inns had been developing slowly over the two and a half centuries between the reign of Elizabeth I and their peak of prosperity at the beginning of Victoria's reign. They had been built and furnished by monks in the Middle Ages to meet the needs of pilgrims, and some of those were so large that they were later adopted as coaching inns. John Twyning and his monks built the 'New Inn' at Gloucester to accommodate 200 of the pilgrims travelling to the shrine of Edward II. The 'George' at Glastonbury was built by Abbot John Selwood about the same time. The 'Angel' at Grantham, which belonged originally to the Knights Templars, was rebuilt in the fourteenth century and given the archway later to be so characteristic of coaching inns, although the front of the building is mainly mid-fifteenth century. Two other famous inns of medieval date, the 'Luttrell Arms' at Dunster, with openings in the stone porch for crossbows, and the 'George' at Norton St Philip in Somerset, were not built for pilgrims. The 'Luttrell Arms' was the town house of the Abbot of Clere, the 'George' was built in 1397 by the monks of Hinton Charter-house for the use of merchants attending the great cloth fair held there.

The first revolutionary change in the typical inn came with the new attitude to creature comforts which manifested itself soon after the Reformation. This liberation from the monastic habit of mortifying the flesh, or of preaching it to the laity, meant that England forged ahead of the rest of Europe in providing standards of comfort that left travellers like Parson Harrison of Radwinter marvelling at the change. The Continent, he wrote, had nothing to compare with our inns. The food, the bedding and fine linen were matters for wonder. The sheets were scented with lavender; ballads and tapestry depicting scenes from the Bible hung from the walls. Blazing fires, good ale, trout fresh from a nearby stream, all combined to make it said that nowhere was an Englishman more himself than while taking his ease with his neighbours in his favourite inn, and that, we may think, is the one basic characteristic of both the Englishman and his inn

29 'The George', Norton St Philip, Somerset

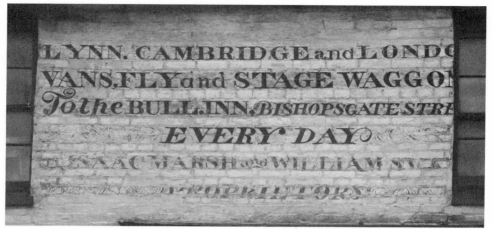

30 A relic of the coaching days from Ely, Cambridgeshire

that has remained constant through every vicissitude of national fortune. So when brewers discuss the need to preserve the character of a house while installing modern conveniences it is of Tudor timbering they are thinking, even if this is only 'Brewers' Tudor' to the initiated. Even Fynes Moryson, who travelled more widely than most Englishmen of his generation, could write: 'The World affords not such Innes as England hath'.

But we must not suppose from this that there was steady progress from that day forward. In fact, the cosy Tudor 'pub' and the great inns of the coaching age belong to different worlds, and Fynes Moryson gives us the clue to the long delay in achieving the posting-house from either the Elizabethan port of call or the hedge-alehouse. It was the roads. He was convinced that English roads were infested with thieves to a greater degree than those of any other country, although he did add that if a highwayman in England got the purses of those he accosted he seldom did them any further injury. In this he may have been over-generous, since nearly a century later, in 1697, orders were given for six able-bodied men to be armed with muskets, carbines, or guns for the protection of east Hertfordshire, and the following year the Lord Chief Justice himself sent out armed men to break up a gang of highwaymen operating from Waltham Forest across the Lea.

The most pronounced difference that developed between the inns of the hospitable and sparsely populated North and those of the wealthy and mobile South was in the charges they made for meals. In the reign of William III it was possible to get a better meal for a shilling in the North than for five in the South. This difference persisted throughout the entire period and accounts for the early fame of the coaching inns on the Great North Road as it passed through Yorkshire. The Hon. John Byng, who must have visited all the best inns in the course of his travels on horseback between 1781 and 1794, was so critical of some well-known hostelries that it would be discourteous to their present excellent hosts to quote him. In the end he got into the habit of sending his servant on ahead to ensure that proper accommodation would be available for himself and his horse when they did arrive, and to avoid the risk of sleeping in a damp bed he carried his own sheets with him. But never was he happier than when he cantered out on to the Great North Road to make his first stop at the 'Sun', Biggleswade, where Mrs Knight governed all with quietness.

John Byng was not the only traveller to send his servant on ahead to check the hospitality that might be expected in the next town. Mr Pickwick sent Sam Weller on to ascertain what kind of hospitality was found at 'The Pomfret Arms', Towcester, and received the report: 'There's beds here. Everything's clean and comfortable. Wery good little dinner, sir, they can get ready in half an hour—pair of fowls, sir, and a weal cutlet; French beans, taters, tarts, and tidiness. You'd better stop vere you are, sir, if I might recommend'.

The high standard to be found in North Country inns was mainly due to their being owned by the local squire, who put in a well-trained butler as landlord, and as the butler had probably married a lady formerly in good service as a cook success was doubly ensured. So when John Byng, who was used to having a butler in unobtrusive attendance, and to having his meals cooked by someone who knew both how to cook and how to carve, dined in small country inns in Yorkshire he found standards being maintained that apparently the South Country innkeepers had never met with. At the 'Spread Eagle', Settle in Ribblesdale, he had an early dinner of beef steaks, lamb chops, pickled salmon and tart, after having for supper the previous night a trout, lamb chops, potted trout, and tart, for which he was charged ninepence for each meal. At the 'White Swan', Middleham in Wensleydale, for one shilling and threepence he dined off boiled fowl, cold ham, Yorkshire pudding, gooseberry pie, loin of mutton and cheesecakes. Small wonder that when he retired for the night he recorded in his Diary: 'A better dinner, and better dress'd, I never sat down to'. So as Yorkshire also bred the best horses and the best ostlers for the stableyards of such inns, the county was well placed to make a name for itself when the coaches rattled in.

But despite what Yorkshire may claim, the great revival of the national spirit that followed the defeat of Napoleon and the triumph of Waterloo centred on London. It was because all the main roads led to London as the hub of the roadway system that we acquired the habit of talking about going 'up' to London, and 'down' to the country. So however important the history of English hospitality as represented in its historic provincial inns may be, the true coaching inn, which flourished for little more than a single generation, was a London creation, and its life-blood was the mail. In a sense, posting houses were alien to the leisurely spirit of the traditional English inn, just as the mail coaches were alien to the spirit of travel as it existed before them, when stops might be made by the wayside, at the request of passengers, for a place of interest to be inspected or a few birds to be shot while the coach was passing through a covert. With the improvement of roads brought about by Telford and McAdam, journeys could be timed to a degree of accuracy impossible when no-one knew at the start how many delays and hazards might be anticipated.

To achieve a timetable large establishments with ample stabling were required in London itself, and conveniently spaced posting houses all long the route at which horses could be changed. Everything, in fact, depended on the availability of good horses. And

PLOUGH HOTEL COACH OFFICE,
Cheltenham.

ROYAL MAILS AND LIGHT & ELEGANT POST COACHES
DAILY TO THE FOLLOWING PLACES.

LONDON MAILS *every Evening at 4 before Six o'clock, thro' Northleach, Burford, Witney, Oxford, Dorchester, Benson, Henty, Salt Hill, Maidenhead, & Hounslow.*

LONDON The Retaliator Coach *every Morning at Eight o'clock, through Northleach, Burford, Witney, Oxford, Tetsworth, Wycomb & Uxbridge.*

LONDON The Two Day Coach *every Morning at Twelve o'clock (Sleeping at Oxford) through Henley.*

OXFORD Coach *every Tuesday, Thursday & Saturday, at Twelve o'clock, through Northleach, Burford, and Witney.*

MILFORD *every Morning at 4 before Eight, thro' Gloucester, Ross, Monmouth, Ragland, Abergavenny, Crickhowell, Brecon, Trecastle, Llandovery, Llandilo, Carmarthen, St. Clears, Narbeth, & Haverfordwest.*

SHREWSBURY & HOLYHEAD *every Morning, except Sunday, at Seven o'clock, through Tewkesbury, Worcester, Kidderminster, Bridgnorth, Cowbridge, Shrewsbury, Oswestry, Llangollen, Corwen, Capel Cerrig, Bangor Ferry, Gwyndu.*

BIRMINGHAM *every Morning except Sunday, at Seven o'clock, through Tewkesbury, Worcester, Droitwich and Bromsgrove.*

BIRMINGHAM & MANCHESTER *every day except Sunday, at Twelve o'clock, through Tewkesbury, Worcester, Bromsgrove Birmingham, Wolverhampton, Stafford, Stone, Newcastle, Congleton, Macclesfield, & Stockport.*

BIRMINGHAM & LIVERPOOL *every day except Sunday, at 4 past one o'clock thro' Tewkesbury, Worcester, Bromsgrove, Birmingham, Wolverhampton, Stafford, Stone, Newcastle, Lawton, (Brereton Green) Holmes Chapel, Knutsford, and Warrington.*

BIRMINGHAM *Monday, Wednesday & Friday, at 4 before Two o'clock thro' Evesham, Alcester & Studley.*

WARWICK & LEAMINGTON *Monday Wednesday & Friday, at 4 before Two o'clock, through Evesham, Alcester, Stratford & Warwick, & returns the following days.*

BATH *every morning, except Sunday, at Nine o'clock, through Gloucester, Rodborough, Petty France, to the York House, from whence Coaches leave daily, to Farrington, Wells, Glastonbury, Bridgwater, Taunton, Wellington, Collumpton, Tiverton, Exeter, Barnstaple, Plymouth, Devonport, Somerton, Longport, Chard, Ilminster, Crewkerne, Axminster, Lyme Regis, Honiton, Sidmouth, Charmouth, Weymouth & all parts of the West.*

BATH *every day, except Sunday, at Two o'clock, through Stroud.*

BRISTOL *every day, except Sunday, at Twelve, thro' Gloster & Newport.*

GLOUCESTER Coaches *at 4 before Eight, Nine, Twelve & Three o'clock.*

SOUTHAMPTON *Monday, Wednesday & Friday, Mornings, at Seven o'clock, through Cirencester, Cricklade, Swindon, Marlborough, Burbage, Collingburn, Luggershall, Werhill, Andover, Werwell & Winchester; in Twelve Hours, & Return the following days.*

THE BERKELEY HUNT, NEW COACH TO LONDON,
every Morning at Six o'clock, through Henley & Salt Hill, to the Castle & Falcon, Aldersgate Street & Belle Sauvage, Ludgate Hill, in 10½ hours; arrives in London at half past Four to Dinner. This Coach leaves the above Houses, calls at the Old White Horse Cellar, & Dyson's Black Bear, Piccadilly, every Morning at half past Six, & arrives at the Plough Hotel Cheltenham, at 5.

PERFORMED BY

JAMES NEYLER & Cº

31 Timetable of coaches from the Plough Hotel Coach Office, Cheltenham here a conflict arose that had to be resolved speedily. If an innkeeper was going to fill his yard with stables, horses, postilions, ostlers and the rest of them, he wanted a return of capital in the increased business he could expect at the bar. But drinking-time meant delay, and delay was the one thing the mail could not allow. The conflict was resolved in the only way possible, which was that the coachmasters, who got their profit from the mail, should either lease or buy the inns along their routes.

Competition between the coachmasters became so keen that many who entered the business went bankrupt in no time, while the successful ones made their fortunes by combining innkeeping with posting and doing both in a big way. The most astute of them was William Chaplin, who in the first quarter of the nineteenth century worked from five London yards of 'Golden Cross' standard, and provided horses for half the London mails on the first stage out and the last stage in. At one time he had 1,300 horses working 60 coaches and 2,000 persons on his pay roll. His chief competitor was a Mr Sherman, the proprieter of the *Shrewsbury Wonder,* the name of a whole service of coaches which from 1825 operated the first long-distance fast coach service. Sherman was able to stand up to Chaplin's competition because he had the advantage of operating from the 'Bull and Mouth' yard directly opposite the General Post Office, and woe betide any man who tried to get in front of him with the mails.

This proprietory dominance of a few large coachmasters led to the architectural convention of all the coaching inns being designed, or redesigned, with tiers of bedrooms along open galleries above the stables, most of which were later cased in. Dickens was always fascinated by these 'galleries and passages and staircases, wide enough and antiquated enough to furnish materials for a hundred ghost stories'. Although the 'Golden Cross' and many other London inns that achieved such fame in the 1830s have gone, 'their double tier of bedroom galleries, with clumsy balustrades running along two sides of the yard', as Dickens describes them, and the yards, in which 'a few boys in smock frocks were lying asleep in heavy packages' or heaps of straw, and where Sam Weller made his first appearance polishing a pair of boots, can no more be demolished than *Pickwick* can.

As with so many of the inns in Dickens there are endless arguments as to which were the originals in *Pickwick Papers.* Some assert that the 'George', Southwark, was the original 'White Hart' in the Borough, to which Jingle and Mrs Wardle were pursued by the lady's father and Mr Pickwick. It certainly has all the atmosphere required; but as Dickens was writing fiction he had no need to keep slavishly to any 'original' and seldom did. I couldn't count the times I have been asked to adjudicate on whether the 'King's Head' at Chigwell or the much less romantic 'Maypole' at Chigwell Row was the original of the 'Maypole' in *Barnaby Rudge.* So I can sympathise with other local historians who are presumed to have proprietory knowledge in such matters. Fortunately, I know the answer that Dickens himself gave to the 'Maypole' question, which was that he 'patched'. In four words instead of one, he produced a composite picture. The 'King's Head' was the building he had in mind; but the 'Maypole' suited his purpose better as a name, and once he had decided on that as a name it was obvious that he must have a green for it, which Chigwell's 'King's Head' lacked.

Tony Weller is credited with operating from 'La Belle Sauvage' at the foot of Ludgate

Hill (the inn from which the Cambridge coach set out), in the famous exchange:

'What's your name, sir?' says the lawyer.
'Tony Weller,' says my father. 'Parish?' says the lawyer.
'Bell Savage', says my father; for he stopped there wen he drove up, and he know'd
 nothing about parishes, he didn't'.

In fact, Tony Weller's coach ran to Ipswich from the 'Bull', Whitechapel, an inn kept
by one of the 'widders' he had learnt to 'beware of'. Her name was Mrs Anne Nelson, and
Charles Harper, who wrote so much on coaches, tells us that she was 'one of the stern,
dignified, magisterial women of business, who were quite a remarkable feature of the
coaching age, who saw their husbands off to an early grave and alone carried on the
peculiarly exacting double business of inn-keeping and coaching proprietorship, and did
so with success'. The other 'widder' in Tony's life, the one who tricked him into
marriage, kept the 'Marquis of Granby' at Dorking, and again no inn existed at Dorking
that fits the picture completely. Claims to the title have been put forward on behalf of
both the 'King's Arms' and the 'White Horse'. All we can say is that of the two the
balance of probabilities would be in favour of the 'King's Arms', although again it could

32 'The Angel and Royal', Grantham, Lincolnshire

only be sustained on the belief that Dickens 'patched'. So we shall never know whether either was accurately described as a house in which 'the bar window displayed a choice collection of geranium plants, and a well-dusted row of spirit phials', or that 'the open shutters bore a variety of golden inscriptions, eulogistic of good beds and neat wines; and the choice group of countrymen and ostlers lounging about the stable door and horse-trough afforded presumptive proof of the excellent quality of the ale and spirits which were sold within'.

When Tony Weller's coach ran from the 'Bull' to Ipswich others ran from the same yard by a different route to Norwich, and Mrs Nelson's coaching interests generally seem to have been extensive. Another London yard that bustled with passengers coming and going was the 'Saracen's Head', where Squeers collected his victims. This stood on the north side of Snow Hill, three doors away from St Sepulchre's Church. It was pulled down when Holborn Viaduct was built about 1868, which was also the date of the demolition of the Whitechapel 'Bull'. West-bound coaches set out from the 'White Horse Cellar', which stood near the corner of Dover Street, and was replaced in 1884 by another house swinging the same sign, but built on the opposite side of the road.

Thousands of horses were needed to service these coaches along the main highways. Ten years before the coaches were speeded up to carry the mail they had already been enlarged so boldly that they were carrying eight passengers inside and ten on the roof. According to the *Annual Register* for 1775 there were 400 coaches on the road and 17,000 four-wheeled carriages. This meant that hundreds of inns had stable-yards with well-appointed services for the hire of chaises and horses, and that travellers who needed neither got short shrift from their owners. Many of the chaises were for those who needed conveyances to carry them to their destination after they had been put down from the coaches. For one service or another we can reckon that 50 to 60 horses would be required to be 'on call' in the yard of the 'head inn' of every market town.

These horses were in the charge of a horsekeeper paid out of their earnings by the post-boys, of whom there would be one for every four horses, two of which would be taken out at a time. When the mail coaches took over, the service was smartened up until the post-boys became as conventionally dressed as the coachmen they attended. They were kitted out —a phrase that came into use with the mails—in short red jackets, or blue jackets with red waistcoats, and corduroy breeches. The jackets had black velvet collars and cuffs, while for headgear they wore tall beavers in contrast to the low-crowned hats of the coachmen. At every posting-inn at least two of these post-boys, booted and spurred, with horses fully harnessed, were to be seen strutting about the stable-yard or chatting up the maids from eight in the morning till seven in the evening.

The hiring of post-boys and horses for private coaches became an expensive business in this newly sophisticated world of fast transport. One of the Norfolk Gurneys recorded in 1822 his surprise as a child on seeing his father pay out so many gold pieces to the post-boys who came up to the window at the end of each stage.

Many new inns were purpose-built for this lucrative business. The Stamford Hotel on the Great North Road (c.1820) is the most imposing example; but there are scores of others, although not every town needed to start from the foundations. Most of the noble families of those days had town houses in the provincial capitals or county-towns that could be adapted. The 'Peacock' at Rowsley had been the dower house for the family at Haddon Hall. Less than five miles away is Bakewell, with the 'Rutland Arms' in the square, where Jane Austen stayed while working on *Pride and Prejudice*. Bakewell is the 'Longstone' of the book and Chatsworth is 'Pemberley'.

Presumably it was when these important town houses of the nobility were being taken over that the painting of inn signs with their arms came into vogue. It certainly seems to have been an eighteenth-century innovation which no doubt was thought to add a certain *cachet* to the house. Such signs would have been useless earlier. The whole point of having a pictorial sign was that it provided a means of identification for those who were unable to read but could recognise such badges as the 'White Lion' of the Howard Dukes of Norfolk, the 'Blue Boar' of the Earls of Oxford, or the 'Bear and Ragged Staff' of the Earls of Warwick. These pictorial symbols warmed their hearts and stimulated their taste-buds as effectively as 'The Angel' of the pilgrims or the 'Saracen's Head' of the crusaders had enlivened travellers in the Middle Ages. And the beauty and elegance of these signs are themselves evidence of their link with a period of aggrandisement. One of the most graceful is to be seen at Wilton, where the three silver lions of the Pembrokes hang from a wrought-iron support fashioned to represent the raised spikes of an earl's coronet. Sometimes a sign that was thought to have lost its meaning was replaced by one of these new heraldic family signs. I don't know when the 'Saracen's Head' at Towcester became the 'Pomfret Arms', but that is the kind of thing that was happening all over England in the great days of coaching. Two signs that definitely reflect the enhanced importance of inns patronised by the coaching fraternity are the 'Lansdowne Arms' at Calne on the Bath Road, which had formerly been a smaller house called 'The Catherine Wheel', and the 'Methuen Arms' at Corsham, formerly the 'Red Lion', which is of special interest because it has a painted chequers sign on the stone posts of the Public Bar entrance. It has been suggested that these counting tables, squared like chess boards, were for easier reckoning of money before tills were invented.

Not all these changes were welcomed by the locals. The spirit of 'Merry England' was not easily extinguished. When the benign countenance of Sir Roger de Coverley was painted on one sign, a local wag converted it back into a scowling 'Saracen's Head'. Perhaps the best instance of local resistance to an attempt to impose respectability on an old-fashioned 'spittoon and sawdust' pub occurred at Ambleside in the Lake District, where an inn called 'The Cock' was bought by Bishop Watson, and as a compliment to the new owner was renamed 'The Bishop' and given a new signboard portrait of his lordship, wig and all. This gave a rival innkeeper the idea of mounting on his own house the sign of 'The Cock', which he did so successfully that he captured the trade of the original. Whereupon the landlord of 'The Bishop', not to be outdone, painted under the Bishop's portrait on his own sign: 'This is the Old Cock'.

The most impressive inn sign in England was the one outside the 'White Hart' at Scole on the Norfolk-Suffolk border, which also housed a round bed that could accommodate 20 couples against the maximum of 12 that could be tucked into the Great Bed of Ware. Some of our inn signs were regarded by overseas travellers as among the 'sights' of England. The German traveller, Karl Phillip Moritz, wrote about 'the amazing signs which, at the entrance to villages, hang in the middle of the street, being fastened to large beams, which are extended across the street from one house to another opposite it, particularly struck me'. Moritz was a German pastor, and not everything in England was to his liking. When the waiter at the inn at Windsor, where he had found little comfort, put out his hand for a tip he was calmly given three halfpence. On which the reverend gentleman records 'he saluted me with the heartiest "God d--n you, Sir!" I have ever heard'. At the door he was further accosted by a maid with '"Pray remember the chamber-maid!" "Yes, yes," said I, "I shall long remember your most ill-mannered behaviour, and shameful incivility"; and so I gave her nothing'.

More important than these asides are the architectural trends that are such revealing commentaries on eighteenth century and Regency social history. After the stable-yards I would put the porches, particularly where a low window at the back opens into a long room that may now be adapted to serve as the dining-room of a good-class hotel—a name that only came into use as an alternative to 'inn' in the third quarter of the eighteenth century. This long room was probably the local 'Assembly Room', where minuets were danced when life was lived elegantly and serenely. Many of these late eighteenth-century inns have 'The George' as their sign. 'The Royal George' at Knutsford always strikes me as trying to improve on the original in the way some local dignitaries try to improve on the dignified simplicity of the loyal toast. But this particular 'Royal George' is entitled to give itself airs since it was patronised by Sir Walter Scott and was where the ladies of 'Cranford' danced and played cards. One of the finest of the Regency inns, and another 'Royal' is the 'Royal Clarence' at Bridgwater, Somerset.

Most market towns have old prints showing the announcements by 'returning officers' of election results or of proclamations being made from the platforms of these Georgian porches, which were sometimes balustraded. Salisbury has an amusing and at the same time impressive reminder of the competition between local hostelries during this period to have the finest porch. It was to assert its superiority to the 'Antelope' that the porch of the 'White Hart' was surmounted by a life-size figure of the noble beast. This is believed to be the inn Dickens had in mind when he described a hall as being 'a very grove of dead game and dangling joints of mutton'.

The two rival houses at Chichester were the 'Dolphin' and the 'Anchor', which finally united so happily under a dual sign. Before that happy consummation their rivalry had been political, with the 'Dolphin' the Whig and the 'Anchor' the Tory headquarters. Evidence of the enmity that existed between them towards the end of the eighteenth century is found in an advertisement which appeared in the *London Star* of 7 July 1792:

'Gentlemen and Ladies travelling in Post Chaises are particularly desired to order Postilions to drive to the 'Dolphin', as various Arts are used to prevent the good intentions of J. Parsons' friends'. We are not told what the various arts were; but Mr Parsons had just come in as landlord. We do, however, know that there was considerable cunning employed in some places to gain the custom of travellers. At Lynton in Devon, for example, postilions would be stationed in the churchyard to spy out coaches descending Countisbury, so that they could gallop down into Lynmouth and offer their services to get them up to the 'Crown' or one of the hotels at the top of the hill. Nor must it be thought that this kind of rivalry died out with the coaching age. It continued in many parts until the Second World War. I remember driving into a small village with

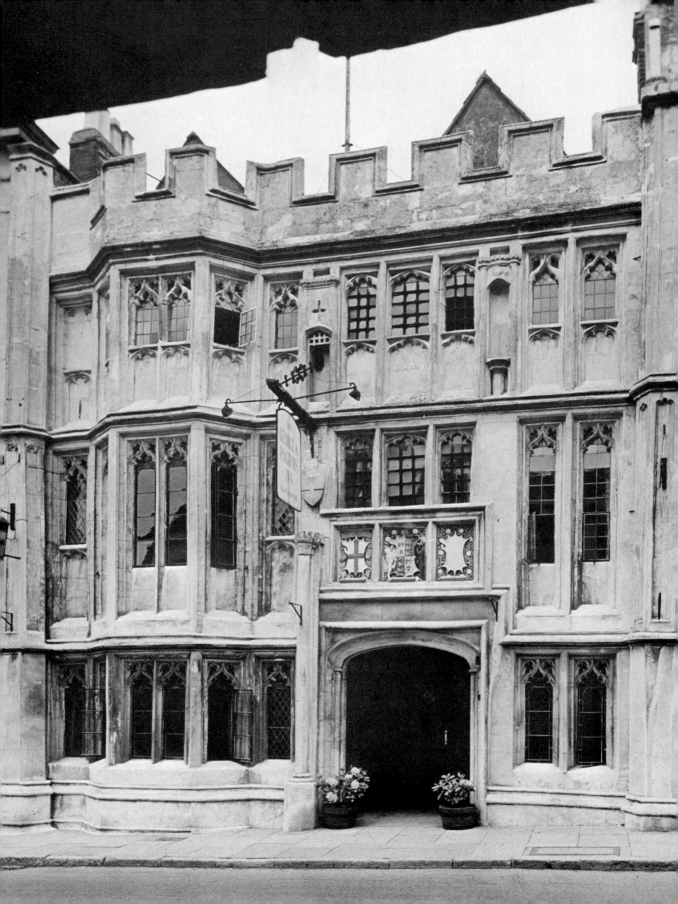

two inns close to each other on the village green 50 years ago and enquiring at the cottage post-office about one that looked extremely clean and attractive. The Postmistress's warning against it was echoed by two or three other locals, all recommending the house that seemed to me to have nothing to commend it. Fortunately I backed my own judgment and found every satisfaction. When the landlord had gained my confidence I told him what had happened and learned that he and his wife were newcomers to the village and had not yet been accepted.

The 'Dolphin' appears to have been a sign imported from France where it is thought to have been a corruption of 'Le Dauphin'. It is found in several English ports, and it would be interesting to know in how many it replaced the earlier 'Chequers' sign, which had been especially popular in ports both for the reason already given and because it often indicated a place where currencies could be exchanged. Be that as it may, the 'Dolphin' became a popular sign in the eighteenth century. Jane Austen, we know, regularly attended dances held in the Assembly Room of the 'Dolphin' at Southampton, where winter assemblies were patronised by royalty. Thackeray is reputed to have written part of *Pendennis* at the 'Dolphin', Southampton, which dates from George III's reign, and asserted its pre-eminence over all the other Dolphins by inserting bow windows claimed to be the largest in England.

The 'Lion' at Shrewsbury is the supreme example of how much influence an inn could exert on the course of a road. It was one of its landlords, Robert Lawrence, who got the Holyhead road diverted through Shrewsbury from its old route through Chester. The achievement is commemorated on his tombstone in St Julian's churchyard. Dickens stayed there in 1838 with his illustrator Phiz, sleeping in what was then an annexe which he described in a letter to his elder daughter; but the glory of the 'Lion' is the Adam ballroom, which reflects all the elegance of its period and all the optimism of its newly found prosperity.

Alas! that prosperity had already reached its peak, and its decline was swift. Probably the last of the great coaching inns to be built in the East of England was the 'Bell' at Saxmundham, Suffolk, in 1842. It can have been very few years later when the 'Old Blue', the last of the coaches that worked the Great Yarmouth Road which the 'Bell' was built to serve, was driven into the yard after completing its last journey, and was left there to rot. We must marvel at the optimism that prompted the building of such an inn in a small East Anglian town in 1842, because in either that year or the next the coaching business was so depressed in London that the yard of the 'Bull and Mouth', where fast coaches had been pioneered and the mail business had been so lucrative, was up for sale. Only three of the 70-odd coaches that had driven out of its yard a few years earlier were left. Only one post-boy was left at Barnby Moor on the Great North Road, and the horses everywhere were in a sorry state. Conditions were so scandalous at the end that teams would be referred to disparagingly as 'three blind 'uns and a bolter'.

Most of the horses were overworked while the business was in decline. Earlier, coachmasters like William Chaplin had been proud of their teams, and had replaced one-third of their horses annually in order to maintain maximum speed for the mails, using a formula for changes of one horse for every mile of road during the winter months with fewer in summer. In some parts of the country the rate of wastage was so great during the

33 'The George and Pilgrims' Inn, Glastonbury

winter months that only summer services were run. Throughout his time that wise old character, Tony Weller, refused to drive his horses as hard as many of his contemporaries did. To the end he continued to maintain a steady pace of eight miles an hour between Whitechapel and the 'Great White Horse' at Ipswich, arguing that by so doing he could keep his horses on the road every night of the year, weather permitting, and expect an average working life of six years from his 'wheelers'.

The collapse of the coaching business was a calamity for towns of similar size to Saxmundham. I know how long it took Epping to recover from its effects. At one time there were 25 coaches rattling along the High Street daily to and from Norwich, Bury St Edmunds, Cambridge and other East Anglian towns. Normally they were drawn by four horses; but it was recorded that in 1820 the *Norwich Times* caused excitement by arriving with six horses and loaded with parcels and turkeys for the London markets. To service these coaches there were 200 horses stabled in the inn yards along Epping High Street. In 1848 only two coaches passed through the town daily. The London to Cambridge line through Waltham Abbey had killed the trade. When the posting-house equipment at one local inn was sold up in 1844, 42 horses with harness, coaches and so forth were put up. Without doubt, hundreds of towns of comparable size retain similar records.

The situation was well summed up by Surtees when he wrote: 'The large comfortable old posting-houses that existed prior to railways have all disappeared . . . or, if any remain, are dragging out miserable existences, with weak worn-out establishments, women waiters, and either antediluvian ostlers or ignorant hobbledehoys fresh at each quarter, who hardly know how to put on a bridle'. In 1846 Thackeray wrote: 'I wonder where they are, those good fellows? Is old Weller alive or dead? . . . Alas! we shall never hear the horn at midnight, or see the pike-gates fly open any more'. How many must have felt as he did!

Ten years later, however, coaches were running again from the 'Golden Cross' by Charing Cross to Brighton, charging thirteen shillings for the journey—'children in lap and outside passengers half-price'. A new craze for sea-bathing and travelling for pleasure had arrived in the nick of time to save both the inns and the roads they served. William Cowper celebrated it in the lines:

> *Your prudent grandmamas, ye modern belles*
> *Content with Bristol, Bath, or Tunbridge Wells,*
> *When health required it, would consent to roam,*
> *Else more attached to pleasures found at home;*
> *But now alike, gay widow, virgin, wife,*
> *Ingenius to diversify dull life,*
> *In coaches, chaises, caravans and hoys.,*
> *Fly to the coast for daily, nightly joys,*
> *And all, impatient of dry land, agree*
> *With one consent to rush into the sea.*

CHAPTER NINE

Touring for Pleasure

❖◆◆◆❖

Dᴜʀɪɴɢ the third quarter of the seventeenth century the steady improvement in roads was already making travel for pleasure possible for those who could afford it as a relief from the monotony of normal life in the country. But those early tourists were of the landowning class, and they studied what they saw as material for landscaping. It was extremely raw material. The countryside had not yet recovered from the long period of decline under the rule of the abbots, recently accelerated by the ravages of the Civil War. The valleys were still undrained except by natural watercourses that were all too liable to flood in winter, giving rise to scores of farm- and field-names signifying swamp or wet. The hills were seen by all but a few virtuosos as uncouth and forbidding. They inspired such names as 'Hunger Hill', 'Starvecrow Farm' and the like. Prospects everywhere were depressing in winter to all except those who travelled in their own phaetons, with blinds that could be drawn to shut out offensive views. From the comfort of their swan's down rugs the wealthy intelligentsia might pass the time indulging in fantasies about shepherds and milkmaids inspired by their reading of the classics, or dream of a Garden of Eden to which sinful man might be restored after completing his atonement for the sins of remote ancestors. Milton, they may have thought, had provided them with a blue-print in *Paradise Lost.* Scenery was not for the uninitiated even at the end of the eighteenth century. The word itself, as applied to landscape, only dates from 1784.

The long road to our modern appreciation of scenery was trodden out in England in one small region: the Lake District, where so much pioneering work was later to be done in conservation. I remember the pleasure I had in blowing the dust off a little book published in 1709 by the Rev. Thomas Robinson, rector of Ousby in Cumberland, who was clearly irritated by the superior tones of those who disparaged mountain scenery. 'Some or our late theorists,' he wrote, ' seem to be of the opinion that the antediluvian earth was mathematically round, without mountains, hills or valleys, as if these exuberances of its surface, like warts and wens, were the deformities of it. But if these new theorists had considered that God had made nothing in vain, but to wise ends, and the best of purposes, though our dark intellect is not able fully to comprehend them, they would have been convinced of their mistake'.

At the beginning of the eighteenth century such views were rare indeed. In 1691 Guy Miege described Westmorland, which was to become the tourists' paradise a century later, as 'one of the worst counties in England'. But to him the great charm of England lay in its not being 'overgrown with wild and unwholesome forests, nor dreadful high mountains'. Hills he required only to be raised high enough to afford the traveller charming prospects, and forests were only to be maintained for the pleasure of hunting. Our own Daniel Defoe, in his *Tour through the Whole Island of Great Britain,* taken between 1724 and 1727, found Westmorland to be a county 'eminent only for being the wildest, most barren and frightful of any that I have passed over in England'. The Pennine fells he found 'all barren and wild, of no use or advantage either to man or beast', and he was amazed that Chatsworth should have been built in the bleak and forbidding Derbyshire dales. The *Tour* continued to be reprinted with these strictures until in the eighth edition, printed 47 years after his death, an admission was inserted that whereas hitherto the northern counties had been regarded as barren and inhospitable wastes, they were now acknowledged to have 'natural beauties'.

This patronising attitude is exemplified in a note made in 1723 on the magnificent prospect of Durham cathedral, the first glimpse of which must make an ineffaceable impression on anyone who sees it today, by the Earl of Oxford who was a close friend of Swift, Prior, and Pope. He said he found 'the whole situation somewhat romantic, but to me not unpleasant . . . but others of better judgement condemn this site, to whose opinion I always submit my own, to my great advantage and instruction'.

As private parks and 'improved' landscapes were the only things worth travelling to see for so many of the early English tourists, it was not until a landscape designer who could break free from French domination came along that this superior attitude to tourism could change. To the social historian fashion has a devastating effect on the relationship of values because it throws everything out of focus. Anyway, the man who broke the spell was Sir John Vanbrugh (1664-1726), whose work is to be seen most notably at Blenheim and Castle Howard. Instead of imposing geometric patterns on the existing landscapes, he reversed the process and moulded his own landscapes round what had been provided by Nature. Lakes were allowed to retain their naturally serpentine banks, and respect was shown to such features as 'an irregular, rugged, ungovernable hill'. Finally, Pope gave the seal of philosophical approval to Vanbrugh's method in an exhortation no less applicable to roads than to buildings. They are the familiar lines in *Moral Essays* beginning 'Consult the genius of the place in all'.

This more natural and spontaneous attitude to scenery, which had been pioneered by Addison in the *Spectator* as well as by Pope, was taken up by the *Gentleman's Magazine,* which not only published articles on touring for pleasure, but in 1746 promoted a survey of the coast of Cumberland. In 1747 an account of a visit to John Peel's Caldbeck fells appeared in the same periodical, followed in 1751 by an article illustrated by a small sketch map of the country between Cockermouth and Honister Pass, into which a new interest was introduced in an account of slates quarried on the Pass being carried to Ravenglass for shipment. Botanical notes were increasingly included in such articles, archaeology became a suitable pursuit for gentlemen, despite the damage they did, and gradually the sphere of interest widened until the people who tilled the soil and tended the cattle came to be seen as creators of the lowland landscape, even if the mountains themselves remained austere and apart. Touring for pleasure was becoming more than a leisure pastime. It was, in fact, become a necessity to every Englishman with the country in his blood, who had to earn his living in the artificial environment of towns and cities. Consequently, roads that had been made to lead into towns, became ever more important as escape routes from them.

It took us a long time to realise how important the human interest of the countryside was. I remember an Indian gentleman saying to me after an announcement that Bow Fell was 2,960 feet high: 'Why do you say how high your hills are? I live 30,000 feet above sea level. Why do you not say that they are so romantic because they are dotted over with the little homes of your people?'

In 1759 this new interest in the use of roads for pleasure got a fillip from the Society of Arts' offer of a subsidy of £100 for a series of one-inch-to-the-mile maps of English counties based on actual surveys. These would have delighted my friend from the Himalayas because they showed not only minor roads but the names of most of the farms. About the same time locally-produced Lake District maps began to appear, showing such roads as one from Whitehaven, where the Lowthers had opened up profitable mines, to Wasdale Chapel and Hawkeshead; and Pennant, in his 1772 *Tour,* adds interest to his account of the roads he travelled along by telling us that some of them were carriage roads made by local gentlemen of means at their private expense, which they kindly allowed visitors to use, adding that the public roads also were well maintained. In fact, all the principal roads in Westmorland had been turnpiked in the 1760s. So at the end of the century the Rev. Robert Housman (ancestor of A.E.), who while minister of a church built by himself at Lancaster wrote a guide to the Lakes, was able to claim that 'perhaps no county in the kingdom can boast better roads than those of Westmorland'.

Not later than 1760 another Lake District parson, Dr John Brown, vicar of Morland, near Penrith, and son of a vicar of Cockermouth, wrote a letter which was widely circulated among university friends—including Thomas Gray and Horace Walpole—and eventually printed with Dalton's *Descriptive Poem addressed to two Ladies at their Return from viewing the Mines near Whitehaven.* This letter was so remarkably perceptive of the essential character of Lake District scenery round Keswick that it is believed to have attracted to the district two very different travellers: Brown's friend, Thomas Gray, the poet, and Arthur Young, the agriculturist.

Gray visited the Lakes in 1769, the year following the publication of Dalton's poem with Brown's letter, and although regarded by the tougher Lakelanders as a mere donnish recluse, he excites those who are sensitive to the true charm of the Lakes by the delight he expresses in the very things that delight them in such phrases as 'the shining purity of the lake, just ruffled by the breeze enough to show it alive'.

Arthur Young travelled to the Lakes up the Great North Road and found its condition good until the Pennines had to be crossed. It then deteriorated. The road at Greta Bridge was 'rough and broken', and as it passed High Force was 'very bad'. The turnpike across Stainmore to Brough, by contrast, was 'a most excellent one, dry, level, and free from loose stones'. So was the road from Penrith over Shap. And of the road from Kendal to Windermere, then in the course of construction, he wrote: 'What is finished is as good, firm, level a road as any in the World'. Most visitors from the South used the same roads. Some, however, left the Great North Road in Yorkshire to continue their journey through Skipton, Settle, Kirkby Lonsdale and Kendal, where the scenery was gentler and more varied. Few at that time came out of Lancashire, where the county roads continued to be bad as the result of the prejudice against turnpikes, and the town streets continued

35 Stage Waggon, early nineteenth century

to be paved with cobblestones, as many of them were at the beginning of the present century.

On reaching the Lakes, Arthur Young's description of the scenery round Keswick was obviously influenced by Brown's; but on entering the North Riding on his way North he had written in a style that any man might find in an old diary discovered in the loft of his family home: 'After traversing a vast range of dreary waste, and shut up in a rocky hollow between two wild hills, you break at once upon a view which cannot fail to be astonishing: you look between two hills on one immense plain, comprehending almost the whole of Cleveland, finely cultivated, the verdure beautiful; and the innumerable enclosures adding prodigiously to the view. In front appears a most picturesque hill, intersected with green hedges, one of the most truly pleasing objects in the world'.

The importance of looking through these old accounts of travel is that they show how attitudes to scenery were changing, and that our old roads, which had developed for purely practical reasons were increasingly becoming means of access to ways of life that previous generations had been silent about. Our industrial civilisation is so recent in relation to the long reaches of the past, and was so exciting in its immediate rewards materially, that it took a long time for it to be realized that we are ourselves part of the natural creation and cannot find health and fulfilment apart from it. This explains why in the early years of landscape appreciation it was the artificial and man-made that people came out into the country to admire. Happily, a new landscape was created for them by two men who to our great good fortune were English of the English and worked with nature, not against it. They were, of course, Lancelot (Capability) Brown and Humphry Repton. Between them they added a new value to our English scenery without offending against its basic character. Repton rightly claimed: 'To improve the scenery of a country, and to display its native beauties with advantage is an art which originated in England'. Under their direction our landscape achieved the reconciliation between Art and Nature that Pope and Addison had pleaded for. They put the seal of confidence on our landscape as surely as Telford and McAdam had put it on our roads.

Like all pioneers they had their detractors. Thomas Love Peacock satirised them in *Headlong Hall,* and Jane Austen—surprisingly perhaps—was definitely anti-Repton, actually naming him in *Mansfield Park.* But then Jane had written satirically as a school-girl that Henry VIII had left the monasteries 'to the ruinous depredations of time' chiefly for the purpose of improving the English landscape. So perhaps she wrote tongue in cheek, as no doubt Owen Chamberlain spoke when he remarked to Brown:

'I wish I may die before you, Mr. Brown'.
'Why so?' asked Brown.
'Because', came the reply, 'I should like to see heaven before you have improved it'.

To recognise what is, and what is not, true to the English spirit as we have come to recognise it in landscape appreciation, we only need to turn to the *Travels* of the Rev. William Gilpin, rector of Boldre in the New Forest, who charms us as a man but bores us as a writer. There are, of course, moments when we can agree with him, as when he approves of hedgerows, favours oaks in preference to other trees, and ventures the opinion that 'the proper appendages of a village' are a winding road, several spreading trees, a rivulet with a bridge and a church spire. We might add a 'pub', but Gilpin would not have approved because 'pubs' bring men into contact with the world of travellers, and he attributed the happiness of the people in the 'rough country' of the Lakes to their having 'no great roads among them; and that their simple villages, on the sides of the lakes, and mountains, are in no line of communication with any of the busy haunts of men'. It was in the busy haunts of men that people lost their vision of Paradise and became soiled by commerce. No doubt it was because of this philosophy that he described Buxton, famous for its waters, as 'in a bottom, in this uncomfortable country . . . surrounded with dreary, barren hills; and steaming, on every side, with offensive lime-kilns. Nothing, but absolutely want of health, could make a man endure a scene so wholly disgusting'.

The scenes Gilpin did admire were those he could describe with such phrases as 'the awfulness of shades', 'the horror of precipices', 'the verdure of hollows', and 'the loftiness of rocks', or in which he could ring such changes in parsonic firstly, secondly and thirdly, as when he distinguished between the lakeland mountain passes by describing that from Ambleside to Brothers' Water as 'the wildest and most picturesque', that by Brough over Stainmore as 'dreary rather than wild', and that by Shap as 'both dreary and wild'. Verbosity, as we should expect, sometimes got the better of him, as when he wrote of Dunmail Raise: 'Nothing could suit such a landscape better than a group of banditti. Of all the scenes I ever saw this was the most adapted to the perpetration of some dreadful deed'.

His parishioners, at all events, had reason to be grateful to him. His writings raised money for a village hall and produced a considerable income after his death, which occurred eight years before William Combe's scurrilous pillory of his excesses in *The Tour of Dr Syntax in Search of the Picturesque,* in such lines as:

> *I'll make a* Tour—*and then I'll* write it.
> *You well know what my pen can do,*
> *And I'll employ my pencil too:—*
> *I'll ride and write, and sketch and print,*
> *And thus create a little mint;*
> *I'll prose it here, I'll verse it there,*
> *And picturesque it everywhere.*

Despite this satire, in 1826, 24 years after his death, a pocket summary of his principles was published under the title of *The Tourist's Companion.* Apparently, the public still wanted to be told what it was proper for them to admire!

The word 'tourist' seems to have made its first appearance in the *Gentleman's Magazine,* June 1789, in announcing the death of Mrs Boswell, 'wife of the celebrated tourist'.* In the same year William Mavor used the title, *The British Tourists,* for a collection of travels, in which most of the travellers were looking for parallels in nature of the landscapes of Lorraine and Poussin. They were satirised by Isaac D'Israeli in *Flim-Flams! or, The Life and Errors of my Uncle and the Amours of my Aunt.* Pedestrianism, he regarded as one of the absurdities of the Age:

'"Romantic delights were mine when I went castle-hunting in Wales", exclaimed a picturesque tourist. "Ah! ye golden hours of venerable antiquity and pictorial nature!"'

The last decade of the eighteenth century brought what might be called the conflict between the subjective and the objective approach to scenery to a climax. The year 1798 saw the publication of *Lyrical Ballads* by Coleridge and Wordsworth. It was also the year in which Uvedale Price, a Whig squire of Foxley, near Hereford, and the friend of Reynolds and Gainsborough, supplemented his *Essay on the Picturesque,* published in 1794. The Dutch painters had shown that conventional beauty and sublimity were not essential in Art. There was a third category, which Uvedale Price called the 'Picturesque', and the test of whether an object that was neither beautiful nor sublime qualified for art was whether it was pictorial. He subscribed to Burke's objective theory, but added the footnote: 'Even when I first read that original work, I felt that there were numberless objects which gave delight to the eye and yet differed as widely from the beautiful as from the sublime'. His neighbour, Richard Payne Knight of Downton Castle, near Ludlow, took the different view that objects were not intrinsically suitable for painting; but could be made so by the artist's capacity for perceiving abstract and

*B. Sprague Aller, *Tides in English Taste,* Harvard University Press (1937), Vol. II, p.204

emotive qualities in them, which he could represent in colour.

This quest for the picturesque in landscape, as well as in common objects, affected tourist attitudes. It was discussed by Southey, writing in 1807 under the pretence of being a Spanish gentleman touring in the English style: 'Within the last thirty years', he wrote, 'a taste for the picturesque has sprung up;—and a course of summer travelling is now looked upon to be as essential as ever a course of spring physic was in old times. While one of the flocks of fashion migrates to the sea-coast, another flies off to the mountains of Wales, to the lakes of the northern provinces, or to Scotland . . . all to study the picturesque, a new science for which a new language has been formed, and for which the English have discovered a new sense in themselves, which assuredly was not possessed by their fathers'.

Southey had reason to know how tourism had invaded the Lake District. He lived near Keswick, and when in 1807 he used the words 'within the last thirty years' he would have in mind that the scholarly Thomas West's *Guide* had been published in 1778, and had run through seven editions by the end of the century. More personally, he would be aware of the heated discussions that had disturbed the peace of the Vale since 1781, when the Regatta, first organised for 'people of fashion' on Bassenthwaite Lake in 1780, had been transferred to his own Derwentwater. 'No breast, however unsusceptible of pleasure', one of the promoters had exulted, 'can be indifferent to that display of every

36 *Char-a-bancs at Hampton Court (from The Illustrated London News, 1849).*

beauty which decks the ancient Vale of Keswick on a regatta day'. The long drawn-out battle between those who loved nature for its own sake, and treasured the quiet traditions of the Lake District, and those who wanted to commercialise the region had begun. The irony was that the fashion which commercial interests were exploiting had been started by donnish antiquaries and dilettante patrons of the arts.

But by the time Southey was writing, the down-to-earth spirit of the North was again asserting itself. In 1787 a Penrith land surveyor named James Clarke, who claimed to know what he was talking about since he had spent his working life measuring up and assessing the value of Lake District properties, and had been born and bred in the district, had published *A Survey of the Lakes of Cumberland, Westmorland and Lancashire.* 'The sublime way of writing', he had warned, 'is not my province. . . . The whole of this outcry against regularity seems to me to have arisen from that cant style of painting which Gilpin and some others have introduced into writing. Not a tree, or shrub, or an old wall, but these gentlemen take measure of by the painter's scale; a poor harmless cow can hardly go to drink but they find fault with a want of grace in her attitude, or a horse drive away the flies with his tail . . . for my own part they put me in mind of nothing so much as those landscapes and figures which boys fancy they see in the sky at sunset'.

Clarke undertook to conduct his readers to places which strangers unencumbered by preconceived ideas about what it was proper to admire might delight in. Although he didn't know it, he was reasserting the principle that all good topographers and local historians subscribe to: 'Consult the genius of the place in all', as Alexander Pope put it, using the word 'genius' in the sense of *genius loci,* the natural character of the place.

At this very time the *genius loci* took possession of the mind of the man who was to become the enduring voice of Cumbria: William Wordsworth. We cannot go into the question sometimes discussed, of whether Wordsworth depended more on the Lake District for his interpretation of life, or the Lake District on Wordsworth for the interpretation of scenery; but much less nonsense would have been talked about Wordsworth's character if he had been seen as so essentially the voice of the land he loved so passionately and knew so intimately. Here we think of him primarily as the author of one of the finest guide books ever written: his *Guide through the District of the Lakes in the North of England, with a description of the scenery, &c. for the use of tourists and residents.*

Wordsworth's *Guide* first appeared in 1810 as the introduction to a series of drawings by his friend, the Rev. Joseph Wilkinson. It reappeared in 1820 as an appendix to his own sonnets on the River Duddon. An independent reprint in 1822 was followed by two reprints in 1823 and 1835 respectively, and since then in editions of the collected works. The Tantivy Press of Malvern published a facsimile of the 1835 edition a few years ago. I have a copy of it and find that it is undated. Only those who have studied the history of the appreciation of scenery in detail can fully recognise what a very fine introduction to the Lake District Wordsworth's *Guide* is. Like my friend from the Himalayas he dismissed the claims of those who rhapsodised about its sublimity and the magnitude of its mountains. He had no more use for 'genteel visitors' than the philistine James Clarke had; but he carried his contempt into the temples that the poetasters had built and broke the tablets of the Rev. William Gilpin. To Wordsworth it was vital that the poet and the nature-lover should see 'Man and Nature as essentially adapted to each other, and the mind of man as naturally the mirror of the fairest and most interesting qualities of Nature', which is not all that remote from what Shakespeare himself had said. Infuriated by the way 'the craving for prospect, immoderate particularly in new settlers' was disfiguring the landscape with buildings that were not in the local style he wrote: 'All gross transgressions of this kind originate, doubtless, in a feeling natural and honourable in the human mind, viz. the pleasure which it desires from distinct ideas, and from the perception of order, regularity, and contrivance. . . . But I would beg of those who are eager to create the means of such gratification, first carefully to study what already exists'. If they did this they would learn to appreciate the fine gradations by which objects singled out for their special qualities merge into each other to produce the varied whole which is so much greater than the sum of its parts. The quest for sublimity was too limited an approach to Nature, and to concentrate on one aspect of a scene was to falsify the whole. In particular, to concentrate on the magnitude of the lakeland fells was to throw the landscape out of focus, which was fatal to the appreciation of its particular type of scenery, which depended more than most 'upon form and the relation of objects to each other'. Again, the moral was: 'Consult the genius of the place in all'.

CHAPTER TEN

A Heritage in Peril

———◆◆◆◆———

Our journey along the old roads of England has come full circle. Under the direction of the Countryside Commission several of the ancient ridgeways we discussed in the first chapter of this book have been reopened as long-distance footpaths and bridleways, with continuous cross-country rights of way for walkers, horse riders and cyclists for distances ranging from 80 miles along the South Downs Way to 250 miles along the Pennine Way. Under the same Authority the Coast paths, which are outside the range of this book, extend even further.

The record of how rights of way over private property have been regained for public use begins with the formation in 1865 of the Commons Preservation Society, later renamed the Commons, Open Spaces and Footpaths Society, to resist attempts to enclose areas of Hampstead Heath and Wimbledon Common. It was followed by the historic intervention of the City of London corporation in the dispute between Thomas Willingale, a woodcutter of Loughton, and the lord of the manor over rights to lop trees and pasture cattle in Epping Forest. I have recorded the progress of the succession of actions in my *Portrait of Epping Forest* (1977), and this is not the place to recount it except in relation to two points; the establishment of rights and the responsibility for safeguarding them.

The case of the Commoners, represented and financed by the City of London, turned on the question of the intercommoning of cattle, which means the right to turn out cattle in one manor and allow them to graze over the entire area of the Forest irrespective of manor boundaries. This right was upheld by the Master of the Rolls on the ground that it predated the division of the Forest into manors and had been exercised continuously 'time out of mind', which meant that any manorial rights that had been gained subsequently were subject to it.

Rights of public access over an area of multiple ownership were more complicated. The Commons Preservation Society was not a property-owning body, and the Government had more than once expressed itself as unwilling to become involved in the safeguarding of rights which they had come to regard as constituting a public nuisance rather than an amenity, particularly as they were exercised so near a densely populated part of the Metropolis, and one that was extending at an alarming rate. But for the generosity of the City in undertaking to buy out the lords of the manors and bear the entire cost of maintaining the Forest for the benefit of the public for all time, it is difficult to see how Epping Forest could have been saved indefinitely from enclosure. The point of recalling this problem of rights over land in multiple ownership is that although it existed in

37 Notice on Spettisbury bridge, Dorset

relation to roads in the distant past it no longer does so. Most metalled roads are now in the care of the County Councils as Highway Authorities, and the protection of sections that might be deemed important for historical or amenity reasons is at the will of the public.

The City of London had Sir Robert Hunter, one of the three founders of the National Trust, to thank for the master stroke of advising the City Solicitor to fight the case for the Commoners of Epping Forest on the single issue of the intercommoning of cattle and the continuous exercise of that right 'time out of mind'. Although the protection of ancient roads had not become a burning issue when the National Trust was founded in 1895, rights of way had. One of my boyhood heroes was Canon Rawnsley, the first honorary secretary of the National Trust, a muscular Christian who must have provoked many a Lake District landowner and magistrate to exclaim: 'Will no-one rid me of this turbulent priest!' He was vicar of Crosthwaite, the mother church of Keswick, a cousin of the Tennysons, and himself a minor poet who produced his sonnet a day as earnestly as a Boy Scout produces his good deed, or a valetudinarian his apple. In the fullness of time *Punch* congratulated him on his 30,000th sonnet. Only a man as vigorous as the Canon could have counted them, let alone have written them.

Canon Rawnsley's congregation adored him. When he announced his intention to demolish an obstruction across a footpath on Latrigg and called on every public-spirited parishioner to accompany him in public demonstration of their wrath, 2,000 stout-

hearted lakelanders, armed with crowbars and any other offensive weapons they could
lay their hands on rallied to his call and marched behind him up the hill.

Before the Canon's death in 1920 motor cars were scaling the Lakeland heights—
often in reverse gear, since it was found that one could usually reach the summit in
reverse when the car petered out in bottom gear. I have frequently done so myself. The
Canon did not live to see the invasion of his beloved Lake District by the motor car; but
the problem of providing for public recreation in the countryside increased so rapidly in
the 'twenties that in 1929 Ramsay Macdonald appointed a committee under the
chairmanship of Dr Christopher Addison, as he then was, to investigate the possibility of
creating National Parks in England and Wales. It reported encouragingly in 1931; but as
1931 was a year of financial crisis nothing was done. Eight years later the Access to the
Mountains Act was passed; but as 1939 was the year of the outbreak of the Second
World War progress was again bedevilled. However, with the end of the war came a
spate of optimistic planning for the Utopia that was thought to be about to open up
before us, despite what had happened to the 'land fit for heroes to live in' that had
disappeared like a mirage after the First World War. So in 1947 the Hobhouse
Committee boldly recommended that 10% of the area of England and Wales should be
designated National Parks, and this time optimism and dedication were rewarded. In

*38 North orbital road from Northmoor Hill near Denham, showing the woodland
reserve presented to the nation by the Road Beautifying Association*

1949 the National Parks and Access to the Countryside Act was passed and under its provisions we got as the first of our National Parks 866 square miles in the Lake District.

The first of the long-distance footpaths to be opened to the public was the Pennine Way, pioneered by that determined North Countryman, Tom Stephenson, who remained undeterred by the opposition that came from local authorities anxious about the effect the public might have on their water-gathering grounds, and the landowners who dreaded the damage that unrestrained hikers might have on the sanctity of their grouse moors. With the Ramblers' Association and a strong body of public opinion behind him he and his associates won through and the Pennine Way, designated in 1951, was officially opened on 24 April 1965.

Meanwhile the Field Studies Council was educating the public in countryside appreciation in centres which now include Malham Tarn House on the Pennine Way, a large house built by Walter Morrison on land first cultivated by the Cistercians of Fountains Abbey, which had later been a shooting box on Lord Ribblesdale's estate. As it is now the property of the National Trust the succession of its ownership might be said to reflect a not untypical progression of use in the North of England.

The English have been remarkably tenacious on their rights of way. Throughout history, when an ancient green through-way was replaced by a metalled highway that deviated from the original track the former route was seldom lost, except where it crossed arable land. It might survive as no more than a footpath or bridleway, not infrequently to merge again into the very highway that had bypassed it. As we have seen, the original tracks from which roads evolved were rights of way and nothing more. They had no determined width, and only by custom a determined track. They ran across waste land that was of little value since there was more than enough of it. Vast areas in the North were still unoccupied when the Normans landed. Stainmore, for example, and the dales that ran down to the Tees from it were not settled until the twelfth century, and the enclosures from unclaimed waste are still commemorated there in such farm-names as Unthank, which means land occupied without being liable to any acknowledgement of ownership or thanks. The high-sounding designation, the King's Highway, did not originally signify in law either a metalled road or a tract of land between walls or fences. It merely denoted a legal customary 'right of passage in the Sovereign for himself and his subjects over another's land.' Even when most of the land was cultivated and a trackway clearly marked, if that trackway became foundrous in bad weather the right of passage permitted users to diverge from it to the extent of 'going through the corn'.

We saw in the chapter on Anglo-Saxon and Scandinavian farm- and market-ways how these were established and used to mark parish boundaries. In seeking to establish whether a track in dispute is in fact an ancient right of way it is often useful to look up tithe-maps, which show the parish boundaries clearly. Normally, however, this is a clue found only in regions of either Anglo-Saxon or lowland Scandinavian settlement. In Norse and Celtic hill country streams are the commonest parish boundaries, and country trackways have frequently to be related to ridgeways marked out by prehistoric barrows, many of which were so firmly established that they continued in use as packhorse trails and drove roads.

The indeterminate width of ancient roads brings home to us the importance of grass verges. The Royal Commission on Common Land (1955-58) dealt with this factor in an appendix to its Report. Nevertheless, since most roads are now fenced off, there might still be doubt about how much of the verge is highway and not merely manorial waste or part of a common. It might be presumed that the owner had fenced off as much as he was entitled to; but this must be a rebuttable presumption since he might have left it open for a perfectly valid reason of his own. If there were ditches cut along the verge, which drained the roadway and were kept clear by the Highway Authority, then those must surely be part of the highway, and if the Highway Authority also cut the grass along the verges and maintained them independently of any agreement with the landowner, it might be reasonable to presume that those also were part of the highway. But when it came to determining as a matter of general principle how much of the unfenced waste along every highway was to be held to be part of it, so many exceptions appeared to arise that the Commission found that as the issue involved mixed questions of law, history, and use there must be many places in which the precise width of the highway verges was in doubt. Ancient customs of use might include grazing rights, which would give them commoner status, and there would undoubtedly be prescriptive rights of access to cottages that could only be reached across these verges.

So when the Commissioners' recommendations were implemented in the Commons Registration Act 1965, which required all common land to be registered, provision was included for objections to be lodged so that each exceptional case could be considered on its merits; but if pleas for exclusion had not been sustained by a specified date the land was registered as common. I had a small personal experience of the kind of difficulty that could arise if an owner of common land through which a highway ran, or the local authority responsible for the maintenance of that highway, failed to register an objection to the registration in time. There must have been many such cases, and perhaps more of genuine cases for exclusion that through local ignorance of the history of a highway or of its traditional use never will be made. Ancient rights, as the Epping Forest Act 1878 showed, may be stronger than the public at large realize.

An instance of this came to light in Suffolk following the implementation of the Countryside Act 1968. Green lanes under the Act were reclassified as footpaths, bridleways and byways, which do not enjoy the protection of lanes, still less of ancient highways. Under this legislation the Suffolk County Council sought to have Marsh Lane, Kessingland, confirmed as a footpath, which was how it appeared on the Council's Definitive Map despite its 20-foot width and the fact that it had been surfaced. The rector of Somerleyton protested that the Council had no power to downgrade this particular road, since it was not a green lane, although now fallen into disuse and overgrown, but historically the main highway to Kessingland harbour. The harbour had lost the status it had enjoyed for centuries, but that, the rector contended, did not affect the status of the highway that had led to it. On advice, the County Council accepted the rector's evidence but submitted that as the objection had not been lodged by the specified date, the Council's Definitive Map had been prepared in good faith and must stand until the time came round for it to be reviewed, when the rector's evidence would no doubt be taken into account.

The rector was not satisfied with this and took the matter further, finally obtaining judgment that a county's Definitive Map could not override the common-law principle 'once a highway, always a highway'. A County Council had no power to close a highway by the simple act of downgrading it. Under the Highway Act 1959 the closure of a highway could only be effected under the authority of an Order of a Minister, normally the Secretary of State for the Environment. It could not be closed by voluntary assent, or be presumed to be closed by non-use.* The rector of Somerleyton had proved a worthy successor in the Cloth of Canon Rawnsley and a long succession of country parsons who have taken their stand against bureaucracy in low or high places. May their line never fail!

Another effect of the Countryside Act 1968 which should have had more publicity than it got, was that green lanes, which often run between ancient hedgerows, were no longer protected from ploughing. Consequently scores of miles of them in counties where arable farming predominates have been obliterated by bulldozers. As many estate boundaries ran down the middle of green lanes there was the loss of those demarcations as well as the more serious loss of a clear right of way that now has no more protection than a footpath. Like a footpath it has to be rolled and 'restored', but no country-lover, let alone local historian, can feel that a rolled track can take the place of a grass road that has grown out of the landscape and acquired over the centuries its own character and ecology.

With the loss of hedgerows on a vast scale in counties like Essex, the landscape has been transformed in places beyond recognition, and we must now depend on Constable and eighteenth- and nineteenth-century landscape painters generally to preserve the record for us. But they tell us nothing about their age. For that we must go to the surviving records of the abbeys. As we have seen, those of the monks of Furness are especially revealing in a landscape that was created by the sheep turned out to graze on the fells by the Norse shepherds and later by the monks, and has remained comparatively little changed ever since. We can not only trace fragments of quickset hedges, carefully defined by the monks as hedges of young hawthorns split down the middle and laid horizontally, that were planted at Ambleside in the thirteenth century, but learn from their records that when the abbots enfranchised their pastoral vassals to make them customary tenants they allowed them to enclose quillets (small crofts) for which they were required to pay encroachment rent.

Many hedgerows in the South must be older than this; but the careful way in which the abbots of Furness defined what they required in a hedgerow brings home to us that the hedging method that has been abandoned in the third quarter of the twentieth century, because we can no longer afford the labour to maintain it, has at least 700 years of history behind it, and probably more.

The favourite hedgerow tree was the elm, giving rise to such place-names as Elmdon and Elmswell, and also to that old country saying: 'Ellum hateth man, and waiteth', prompted by the fact that because it lacks a tap root the elm is liable to fall when least expected. In the Lake District the ash was the favourite hedgerow tree, and produced place-names beginning with 'Ash' or 'Ask', its Scandinavianised form. At the approach

*See article in *Country Life,* April, 1977

of winter the branches were lopped off and strewn on the ground for browsing cattle. When the leaves had gone the branches were used for repairing the fences from which they had been lopped. On Exmoor, at the other end of the moorland belt that runs down the whole of the West of England, the only tree that will survive the hard winters is the beech. That is why we find miles of beech hedges planted after much trial and error in the selection of hardy species by the Knight family when they made their enclosures in the nineteenth century. And the Knights of Exmoor, incidentally, were related to Richard Payne Knight, the art connoisseur. Both were members of the Shropshire iron-masters family, who must have used up vast quantities of timber in their furnaces, which had been established in Cromwell's time.

Although hedges defining parish boundaries go back to Saxon times, most of those in the Midlands date from the enclosure awards of the last decade of the eighteenth century and the first of the nineteenth, and were planted to define new estate boundaries just as so many centuries earlier the monks had planted quick along the ancient boundaries of the manor of Coniston, 'the king's manor', in order to separate its enclosures from the common lands on Furness Fell. And although Capability Brown removed them from the estates he landscaped for the Whig nobility, he himself sold thousands of hawthorns from his estate at Fenstanton in Huntingdonshire for these new enclosures. So, as a matter of plain fact, as W. E. Tate said in *The Village Community and the Enclosure Movement,* 'the hedge, the fence, and the wall are the makers of modern rural England'.

If that is so—and it is—has the time not come for pressure to be put on all Highway Authorities to exercise the powers they possess to protect those sections of their ancient byways that they are advised are the most valuable, either as irreplaceable records of local life or for present-day amenity? Before the Industrial Revolution most of the people living in the country were employed on the land, and what we have now formulated as a 'Country Code' was unnecessary. The rules embodied in it were ingrained in the folk who tilled the land and used its roads and footpaths. Ancient use was quite as strong as statutory right. When evidence was taken from the lords of the West Essex manors for the purposes of the fight to saving Epping Forest from enclosure, landowners like the Rev. Robert Boothby Heathcote and George Palmer said that it had never entered their heads to question the use that people made of the waste land within their manors. They liked to see people enjoying themselves.

The differences between their day and ours are much too great to draw morals from their easy-going attitude. There was no talk about maximising land-yield a hundred years ago, when 50% of the population worked on the land. Today, only 1% work the land, striving as hard as they can to produce as much food as possible for the 99% who work in the towns. Consequently industrialisation has invaded rural economy to an extent that even Ruskin, with all his gloomy forebodings of what would happen if it did, never imagined in his worst nightmares.

Financially it may be a good thing that Insurance Companies are now investing pension funds in land, and stockbrokers are becoming week-end farmers with an eye to the increase in value that the land must acquire if inflation continues. There are doubtless both good and bad aspects of these changes, just as there were pluses and minuses in the eighteenth-century enclosures that writers used to get so worked up about. But the concept of 'once a highway always a highway' could hardly be expected to make as much sense to a business man turned countryman as it made to the rector of Somerleyton or as it makes to me. The business man would argue with sound logic from his point of view, that as so many ancient tracks came into use for purely functional reasons that have ceased to apply there is no longer any justification for them. When that argument is put forward, conservationists must be ready to make the point that although ancient tracks came into being for functional reasons that no longer apply they also served amenity purposes. In other words, although little may have been said about it, country folk always used these ancient rights of way for pleasure as well as profit. There is abundant evidence for this in literature, notably in the writings of poets like John Clare, William Cowper, and Thomas Hardy no less that than in those of Wordsworth and his fellow members of the Romantic School. Despite the splendid work done by the Ramblers' Association and other bodies there can be no doubting that many ancient rights of way are disappearing through lack of vigilance. I not infrequently get letters from friends, who on moving away from the Epping Forest area into the country on retirement, are surprised to find that there are fewer walks to be taken from their new home than from their old home near London.

Under the Road Traffic Regulation Act 1967 it became possible for the Highway Authority through whose area a bridleway passes to restrict its use to pedestrians, horses, and agricultural vehicles. It was a power that proved to be less helpful to pedestrians than expected because it was found that if restriction orders were imposed there would be isolated cottages and small-holdings with no means of access for essential services. And when a green lane or cart road classified as a bridleway was found to be a highway by virtue of being ancient ridgeway with public road status, a major complication came to light. In 1978 Lord Foot complained in the Upper House that the great Berkshire Ridgeway from Amesbury to Streatley on the Thames was in danger of suffering irreparable damage from being used by motor vehicles as a highway. As the Berkshire Ridgeway is intersected by metalled roads it has open access for motor cyclists who want to use the whole of it as a rough track, and for motorists who want to use it for short distances as car park or picnic ground.

At the time of writing, the problem posed by this use by motor vehicles of trackways that for thousands of years were used only by men and the beasts they drove along them remains unresolved. After imposing a traffic restriction on a section of ridgeway near Uffington in 1975 Oxfordshire County Council set up a public enquiry to see how the restriction was working. To their embrarrassment the Inspector included in his Report the statement: 'I cannot see how the presence of motor vehicles can affect the conservation or enhancement of the natural beauty of the area'. In the hope of getting the effect of the Inspector's opinion reversed the Countryside Commission has appointed a field officer to investigate and report on what is happening.

With the same object of protecting old wayfaring routes—to use a phrase that so far as I know has not acquired a new legal definition—Essex County Council in 1974 resolved to designate 120 miles of minor roads in the rural north-west of the county 'protected lanes'. This was followed by a similar designation of a further 180 miles over the rest of the county, and an expressed intention to add other lengths after a professional survey and local consultation. As all were unclassified metalled roads under the control of the County as Highway Authority, neither the problems relating to bridleways on the one hand, nor to ridgeways that retained the status of public roads on the other could apply, and local landowners, farmers and District Councils co-operated because they were glad to gain protection from the heavy vehicles that were increasingly using the winding Essex lanes as short cuts to the Thames Tunnel or county airports.

In December 1976 the success of these designations prompted the County Planning committee to hold a conference on the future of 'Rights of Way in the Essex Country-side', based on a discussion paper with that title prepared by the officers of the department, and chaired by Mr Gerald Curtis, chairman of the Planning Committee, who had studied countryside problems in great depth and knew his county. As a practical farmer himself he was able to get the right balance struck between commercial and amenity interests, and create the atmosphere for discussing constructively the question of protecting rights of way over land that was already being cultivated to obtain the maximum yield. As Essex has always been to the fore in recording and signposting foot-paths and rights of way, and its farming is predominantly arable, it was a good county in which to try to foresee the full impact of what was happening and try to reconcile it with the protection of amenities.

I don't know how many similar conferences have been held in other counties. I mention ours because it again brought home to me that this is a problem that cannot be solved at Whitehall because it only becomes real when it becomes local, and that if we are to tackle the question of how to protect our byways as effectively as the pioneers of the National Trust and other bodies I have mentioned tackled their problems, we must start at local level. It must also be recognised that the production of convincing evidence for the protection of ancient highways and byways entails enquiries in much greater depth than that for privately owned buildings that can be seen, measured, and their values assessed in relation to sales. Nor is the evidence of use by local inhabitants, valuable as that may be, nearly enough, I know from experience how often that kind of evidence can be conflicting where it is based on nothing more substantial than memory, and possibly hearsay. The help of the local history societies needs to be enlisted to examine adequately eighteenth-century county maps, estate maps and the like.

To a limited extent this has been done in Essex, and the County Planning officers are doing a complete survey of the roads under county control. But there is a limit to what such a survey can prove, especially where questions of history and use come into the reckoning. In Essex, for example, the County officers have already learned that a section of Roman road is incorporated in Beards Lane, Clavering, which is now classified as a bridleway; that the 'mere' way which follows the line of the parish boundary between Margaretting and Stock has an alignment which suggests that it was formerly used as an alternative route along the Chelmer Valley when the main London road became impassable, and that at Gibbets Cross, near Thaxted, the fact that the land on one side of the road is so much lower than that on the other indicates shifting of the soil due to lynchet cultivation on one side only. These are all examples of clues to ancient uses discussed in the chapters of this book—and, incidentally, the road at Gibbets Cross is a hollow way.

The same kind of clues will be found in every part of the country, but in associations that are uniquely significant in the local history of the parishes in which they occur. So far as lanes for protection are concerned, they must surely be those with local style that developed organically out of the local landscape and its land uses. The question of how those uses came to be lost would be relevant in some places. In one of the Essex lanes mentioned above drainage made its use no longer necessary. When the Midlands were replanned in the eighteenth and early nineteenth centuries many historically important roads must have gone out of use. Some of these survive as blind lanes, and can be spotted from the railway by anyone who carries a pocket atlas with him as he travels. In the North of England, innumerable bridleways used by families on fellside farms for neighbourly visiting have gone out of use with car ownership and the improvement of roads.

These are all circumstances that can only be investigated locally. The co-operation of the farmers and landowners of the present generation could be counted upon. They would either have used them themselves or have heard of former uses from parents or grandparents. Conservation is in their blood. But with changes in ownership from personal to corporate gaining momentum so rapidly, and control becoming increasingly remote, these memories may fade more quickly than we realize. The protection of ancient roads, therefore, both for amenity purposes, and as historical and archaeological records, calls for high priority.

Bibliography

Albert, W., *The Turnpike Road System in England,* Camb. Univ. Press, 1972

Allcroft, A.H., *Earthworks in England,* London, 1908

Allcroft, A.H., *Downland Pathways,* London, 1934

Allen, B.Sprague, *Tides in English Taste,* Harvard, 1937

Anderson, R.M.C., *The Roads of England,* London, 1932

Andrews, W., Bygone England Series, London, 1890s

Balchin, W.G.V., *The Making of the English Landscape: Cornwall,* Hodder and Stoughton, 1955

Baring, F.H., 'William the Conqueror's March through Wessex', *Hants Field Club,* Vol.VII, Pt.2 (1915)

Belloc, Hilaire, *The Old Road,* T.Fisher Unwin, 1904

Belloc, Hilaire, *The Road,* 1923

Beresford, M., *New Towns of the Middle Ages,* Lutterworth Press, 1967

Bland, D.S., 'The Maintenance of Roads in Medieval England', *Planning Outlook,* Vol.IV pp 5-15

Bonser, K.J., *The Drovers,* Macmillan, 1976

Bridbury, A.R., *England and the Salt Trade in the Later Middle Ages,* Ox.Univ.Press, 1955

Burke, Thomas, *Travel in England,* Batsford, 1942

Burton, S.H., *Exmoor,* Hale, 1974

Byng, Hon. John, *The Torrington Diaries,* ed. C.B. Andrews, 4 vols, London, 1934-38

Chanter, J.R., 'Devonshire Lanes', *Trans. Dev. Ass.,* 1873

Chope, R.Pearse, *Early Tours in Devon and Cornwall,* David and Charles, 1978

Clark, Grahame, *Prehistoric England,* Batsford, 1940

Clay, R.C.C., 'Prehistoric Ways', *Antiquity,* Vol.1, 1927

Close, Sir Charles, *The Map of England,* Peter Davies, 1932

Cobbett, William, *Rural Rides*

Coddrington, G.T., *Roman Roads in Britain,* S.P.C.K., 5th edn. 1928

Collingwood, R.G., and Myers, J.N.L., *Roman Britain and the English Settlements,* Ox. Univ. Press, 1937

Collingwood, W.G., *The Lake Counties,* Dent, 1902 (revised edn. 1932)

Copeland, John, *Roads and their Traffic, 1750-1850,* David and Charles, 1968

Copley, Gordon J., *The Conquest of Wessex in the Sixth Century,* Phoenix House, 1954

Copley, Gordon J., *An Archaeology of South-East England,* Phoenix House, 1958

Countryside Commission Publications on Footpaths and Bridleways

Cox, H.Hippisley, *The Green Roads of England,* Methuen, 3rd Edn., 1927

Crawford, O.G.S., *Man and his Past,* Ox.Univ.Pres, 1922

Crawford, O.G.S., *The Andover District,* Clarendon, 1922

Crawford, O.G.S., *Archaeology in the Field,* Dent, 5th imp., 1970

Crofts, J., *Packhorse, Waggon and Post, Land Carriage and Communications under the Tudors and Stuarts,* Routledge and Kegan Paul, 1967

Crosher, G.R., *Along the Chiltern Ways,* Cassell, 1973

Crump, W.B., 'Saltways of the Cheshire Wiches', *Trans. Lancs. and Ches. Ant. Soc.,* Vol. LIV (1940)

Cunnington, M.E., *The Archaeology of Wiltshire,* Devizes, 1934

Curwen, E. and E.C., 'Sussex Lynchets and Associated Field Ways', *Sussex Arch. Coll.,* Vol. LXIV (1964)

Darby, H.C., *The Domesday Geography of England,* Camb. Univ. Press, 1952

Darton, F.J., *The Marches of Wessex,* London, 1936

Defoe, Daniel, *A Tour through England and Wales* in *A Tour through the Whole Island of Great Britain,* Dent, 1962

Dines, H.G., *The Metalliferous Mining Region of South-West England,* H.M.S.O., 1956

Dodd, A.E., and E.M., *Peakland Roads and Trackways,* Buxton, 1974

Donne, W.B., *Old Roads and New Roads,* London, 1852

Duckham, B.T., *The Transport Revolution,* 1750-1830, Hist. Soc., 1967

Dutton, Ralph, *Wessex,* Batsford, 1950

Emmison, F.G., 'First Projected Turnpike', *Bull. of Inst. of Hist. Res.,* Vol. XII, pp. 108-112

Fiennes, Celia, *Journeys,* Cresset Press, 1947

Fordham, Sir Herbert, *The Road Books and Itineraries of Great Britain,* 1570-1850, London, 1924

Gay, Edwin, 'Arthur Young on the English Roads', *Quar. Jour. of Econ.* Vol. XLI (1927)

Gibb, Sir Alexander, *The Story of Telford,* London, 1935

Good, Ronald, *The Old Roads of Dorset,* Dorchester, 1940

Goodwin, H., 'Prehistoric Wooden Trackways of the Somerset Levels', *Proc. Prehist. Soc.,* New Series, Vol. XXVI

Gould, S. Baring, *Old Country Life,* 1889

Gregory, J.W, *The Story of the Road,* Maclehose, 1931

Grundy, G.B., 'The Evidence of Saxon Land Charters on the Ancient Road System of Britain', *Archaeological Journal,* 1917, 1918

Hall, Donald J., *English Medieval Pilgrimage,* Routledge and Kegan Paul, 1965

Halliwell, J.O., *A Dictionary of Archaic and Provincial Words,* Routledge, 1904

Harper, C.G., *Stage Coach and Mail in Days of Yore,* 2 vols., 1903

Harrison, Wm., *Description of Britain,* 1586

Harrison, W., 'The Development of the Turnpike System in Lancashire', *Trans. Lancs. and Chesh. Ant. Soc.,* Vol. IV, pp80-92; 'Preturnpike Highways in Lancashire and Cheshire', Vol IX, pp. 101-134; 'Turnpike Roads in Lancashire and Cheshire', Vol. X, App. ii; 'Ancient Fords, Ferries and Bridges in Lancashire', Vols. XII, XIII; 'Ancient Fords, Ferries and Bridges in Cheshire, Vol. XIV.

Hart, C.R, *The Early Charters of Eastern England,* Leicester Univ. Press, 1966

Hawkes, C.F.C., 'Old Roads of Central Hampshire', *Hants. Field Club,* Vol. IX, Part 3 (1925)

Heath, Sidney, *Pilgrim Life in the Middle Ages,* London, 1911

Helm, P.J., *Exploring Prehistoric England,* Hale, 1971

Henderson, Charles, and Coates, H., *Old Cornish Bridges, Old Devon Bridges,* 1928

Hindley, Geoffrey, *A History of Roads,* Peter Davies, 1971

Hodge, Edmund W., *Enjoying the Lakes,* Oliver and Boyd, Edin., 1957

Hogg, Garry, *Facets of the English Scene,* David and Charles, 1973

Hoskins, W.G., *The Making of the English Landscape,* Hodder and Stoughton, 1955; Pelican Books, 1970

Hoskins, W.G., *Local History in England,* Longman, 1959

Houghton, F.T.S., 'Saltways', *Trans. Birm. Arch. Soc.,* Vol. LIV (1932)

Hussey, Christopher, *The Picturesque,* Frank Cass, 1967

Jennett, Seán, *The Pilgrims' Way,* Cassell, 1971

Jervoise, E., *The Ancient Bridges of England,* Architectural Press, 1930-32

Jusserand, J.J., *English Wayfaring Life in the Middle Ages,* T. Fisher Unwin, 1889

Leland, John, *Itinerary in England and Wales,* c. 1535-43, ed. L.T. Smith, Centaur Press, 1962

McDonnell, J., and Cowley, W., 'Traditions of a Drovers' Road', Country Life, Vol. CXXIX (1961)

Malins, Edward, *English Landscaping and Literature,* Ox. Univ. Press, 1966

Margary, I.D., *Roman Roads of Britain,* Phoenix House, Revised Edn. 1967

Margary, I.D., *Roman Roads in the Weald,* Phoenix House, 1948

Metcalf, John, *Life of John Metcalf ... 'Blind Jack of Knaresborough,'* York, 1795

Moritz, Charles, *Travels through Several Parts of England,* London, 1782

Ogilby, John, *Britannia,* 1675

Oliver, Jane, *Ancient Roads of England,* Cassell, 1936

Page, Wm., 'Notes on the Types of Villages and their Distribution', *Antiquity,* 1927

Parkes, Joan, *Travel in England in the Seventeenth Century,* Ox. Univ. Press, 1925

Peake, Harold, *Prehistoric Roads,* Arch. Cambr. 6th Series, Vol. XVII (1917)

Pelham, R.A., 'The Gough map', *Geog. Mag.* 1933

Pollard, E., Hooper, M.D., and Moore, N.W., *Hedges,* Collins, 1974

Radley, J., 'Peak District Roads Prior to the Turnpikes Era', *Derb. Arch. Soc. Jnl*

Raistrick, A., 'Roman Remains and Roads in West Yorks'. *Yorks. Arch. Soc. Jnl.* (1933);
        Green Tracks on the Pennines, Clapham, 1962

Regions of the British Isles, all volumes

Rolt, L.T.C., *Thomas Telford,* Longman, 1958

Scott-Giles, C.W., *The Road Goes On,* Epworth Press, 1948

Sheldon, Gilbert, *From Trackway to Turnpike,* Ox. Univ. Press, 1928

Stenton, F.M., *Anglo-Saxon England,* Ox. Univ. Press, 1947

Stenton, F.M., 'Medieval England', *Econ. Hist. Rev.,* Vol. VII (1936-37)

Stroud, Dorothy, *Humphry Repton,* Country Life, 1962

Stukeley, Wm., *Itinerarium Curiosum,* 2nd edn., 1776

Tate, W.E., *The Village Community and the Enclosure Movement,* Gollancz, 1967

Thomas, Edward, *The Icknield Way,* Constable, 1913

Thoresby, Ralph, *Diary,* 1830

Thorpe, H., 'The Green Villages of County Durham, *Proc. of the Inst. of Brit. Geog.,* 1951

Timperley, H.W., and Brill, Edith, *Ancient Trackways of Wessex,* Phoenix House, 1965

Tristram, W.O., *Coaching Days and Coaching Ways,* Macmillan, 1961

Webb, Sidney and Beatrice, *English Local Government; The Story of the King's Highway,* London, 1922

Wilkinson, T.W., *The Highways and Byways of England,* London, 1913

Williams, Michael, *The Draining of the Somerset Levels,* Camb. Univ. Press, 1970

Wright, Thomas, *The Celt, the Roman and the Saxon,* London, 1852

Young, Arthur, *A Six Weeks Tour through the Southern Counties of England and Wales,* London, 1768

Glossary

agger a mound; the raised track of a Roman road; the rampart of a Roman camp

anstey a narrow uphill footpath; the name of hillside places in six counties

argin an embankment; a rampart

argolet a light horseman; plural: argoletiers

arval a funeral feast at which arval bread is eaten (North of England)

badger corn factor; buyer of butter, eggs, &c. at farmhouses; originally a licensed beggar

baggabone a vagabond

bagman commercial traveller—originally so-called because he carried his samples in saddle-bags

bail the half-hoop for supporting the cover of a waggon; in North of England a beacon or bonfire

bank slope of a hill; vernacular for 'nab' or 'scar'

bar a barrier; a turnpike; in York and elsewhere a gate

bargh bridleway up a steep hill (North of England)

barth a shelter for cattle

barway a passage into a field between removable bars or rails

bayard a bay horse (French)

beard-hedge the bushes stuck into the bank of a newly planted hedge for protection

beau-traps loose pavements in a footpath under which dirt and water collected to splash anyone who trod on them

bedlam-beggars half-witted vagrants

beggars-bush a rendezvous for beggars

belfry a temporary shed for carts or cattle formed by four posts erected to support a thatched roof

bermudas cant term for obscure alleys in which cheap lodging could be found. The name is given to narrow passages in Covent Garden

boles places in hill country where ore was smelted; bee skeps

boonmaster waywarden

borrans heaps of stones along a Roman road; burial places

borstal, bostal, burstel pathway up a steep hill

bough-houses private houses open for the sale of liquor during fairs, when an ivy branch would be hung over the door; also called Ivy-bush houses

brogger licensed pedlar in wool; jobber; broker

broggs, brogs staves stuck into a swamp to mark a track (North of England)

broomway road marked by stakes of broom

cadators beggars who travelled in the guise of decayed gentlemen—apparently derived from cad

carfax a meeting of four ways (Oxford)

carrefour as carfax

carse alluvial land along a river bank (North of England)

carvet a clipped hedge, probably derived from carve (Kent)

caulk chalk, limestone

cahsy, carsel, causey causeway, or raised road across land liable to flood

cawnse a pavement (Devon)

cepe hedge

chare, chore a narrow lane or wynd

chewar, chewer as chare

church-litten churchyard

chute shoot; a steep slope or cutting

clap-gate a flapping gate to save horse-riders having to dismount

clap-stile a stile with movable horizontal steps

clapper-stones a bridge of stone slabs

cobbles round stones for surfacing roads

cop summit

corpseways tracks along which the dead were carried for burial. Also *lykeways*

delf, delph a quarry

dimensurator seventeenth-century instrument for measuring road distances

dole-stones landmarks indicating the divisions of moors or common land

dorsel a packsaddle; panniers in which fish was carried on horseback

dowels marshes (Kent)

dowt a ditch (Lincs.)

drag a fence or hurdle suspended from a pole across running water

drang, drong alley (Dorset) a word used by William Barnes, the Dorset poet

droke alley (Herts)

driftway track along which cattle were driven

edge local name for faulted sides of the Pennines

Essex-stile a ditch

falgang a gang of beggars

fall-gate a gate that can be dropped across a public road

farman a hawker; pedlar (North of England)

farrow a wayfaring; a path

faw an itinerant tinker; potter, &c. (North of England)

faw-gang a gang of faws

fearn a windlass (Lincs)

feather-bog a quagmire

flagging stone paving (North of England)

flam low marshy ground

flawes squares of peat, called 'flights' in Lancashire

folly footpath (Colchester)

forks gallows

fostal a paddock or the way to it

fusterer a maker of packsaddles

gadling a vagabond

gad-whip an ox-whip

galley, or *gallox bridge* packhorse bridge, from galloway

galloway a small horse of 15 hands used in packhorse trains. In Durham pit ponies were called galloways

gang-days rogation days when the parish boundaries were perambulated—'ganging' being North of England for going

gangerel a vagabond

gangway an entry or passage

gannoker a tavern- or inn-keeper

garrant a gelding

gate road (North of England)

gatteram a green lane (Lincs)

gauk Rochdale form of 'ginnel'

gild village green (North of England)

ginnel a narrow passage (Lancs.)

gout the gateway bridge over a water course or sluice (Warw.)

greenhew tribute paid to landowners in Westmorland for permission to cut boughs of trees

greenstone the slatey rocks of Cornwall

grip a drain or ditch

gruffs lead mines (Mendips)

gut a wide ditch or water course that discharges into the sea

haggler the upper servants of a farm (Isle of Wight)

halterpath a bridleway

handling-post early signpost, so called from being in the form of outstretched arms with pointing hands

hatch forest gate

hayment a boundary or fence

hebble a small plank bridge

hedge-alehouses country alehouses where drovers and poor travellers could sleep on haylofts in barns or in the stage-waggons in which they were travelling after refreshing themselves in the alehouse

helm summit of a hill, or crest of a long narrow ridge

heugh a precipice, cliff or crag

higgler one who higgles or haggles in bargaining over dairy prices

hipping stones stepping stones (North of England)

hirsel a flock of sheep (Cumb.)

hoar-stones stones marking divisions between estates or parishes

hock-cart harvest-home cart; the last loaded waggon

hoggin the sand sifted from gravel before the stones were spread on the road

hollow way a way lower than the surface of the adjoining land, normally as a result of rain washing away the surface soil

holy stone a stone with a natural hole through it, believed to be a charm against witchcraft

hook-seams panniers (North of England)

intake land taken in from the common

ivy-bush see bough-houses

jagger hunter, from the German *jaeger;* adopted for both the driver of packhorses and the man who stabled them for hire

jazzup, jubbin donkey

jigger alley (Liverpool)

jobber usually yarn jobber

jowler alley (Liverpool)

jugglemear, jugglemire swamp or bog (Devon)

kegway smugglers' way (kegs of brandy)

keld spring, well (Craven)

kipped fenced, hedged (Devon)

kyloes a small breed of Highland cattle

lade ditch or drain (origin of Ladbrook)

lagger, lugger green lane

lanebegot bastard

lidgetts gates set up at the end of villages in the Isle of Oxholme and elsewhere to prevent cattle straying on to arable land

lineway a straight direct path

links sandy grass-covered land near the sea shore

loadmen carters

loan, lonning lane or byway between hedges. In the North of England a loaning could be a place used for milking cows

lodes Fenland ditches and drains

loke path (Norfolk)

lone lane (West Midlands)

lychgate the churchyard gate, roofed to shelter bearers of the bier until the parson came to meet them and read the introductory part of the service for burial before leading the funeral procession into church

lykeway corpseway

maer-wegs boundary ways in Saxon charters: *maere* and *gemaere* were originally used as names for balks

mear, mere boundary bank or hedge; *mere-stones,* boundary stones. Mere is a boundary town

mews originally a place where hawks could mew or moult. When falconry declined it came into use for stabling

mimmam bog (Brk.)

murgin bog (Chesh.)

nickopit bog (Kent)

outrake a path along which sheep were driven on to the northern fells

owlers smugglers who carried wool to France illegally by night

ox-gang area of land to be cultivated by one ox

packgate a gate on a back lane

packway packhorse trail

pallant palace enclosure; the south-eastern quarter of Chichester

palliser maker of palings or fences—palisades

pardoner frequenter of Pilgrims' Way selling pardons and indulgences

parvis church porch used by lawyers for consultation

patrics cant term among beggars for hedge priests

peatway track along which peat was brought down on sledges from the moor

pennock a small bridge over a water course (Sussex)

peth a road up a hill (incorporated in Morpeth)

plashing lowering a hedge by cutting off the pleach branches and entwining them

polder marshy tract (Kent)

pontage bridge toll

pucksey quagmire, probably from the belief that Puck might lead travellers into bogs

quag, quabbe, quakemire all words for quagmire

quenchy wet, swampy

quick growing plants set for a hedge

quob quicksand

rab a kind of loam; a coarse hard substance for repairing roads in Cornwall

racke, rake a path, range, or walk for sheep or cattle. Rake is a common name for a sheep-dog in the Lake District

racket passage between walls (Beverley)

rain ridge

raine a strip of unploughed land round an arable field, or between the divisions of old common fields

raise cairn of stones (Dunmail Raise)

randies itinerant beggars and ballad mongers

ratchel gravelly soil

releet a crossing of roads

repple a long walking staff as tall or taller than the bearer

ridding clearing

ride a way through a forest or wood

ring-fort round area surrounded by banks and ditches

rise-dike a hedge made of boughs and twigs

scoanes, sconce stones, pavement (Cornwall)

score a cut through a declivity (Lowestoft)

shireway bridleway

skid a hook fixed to the wheels or axle of a waggon to prevent it running downhill too quickly

skid-pad a shoe fixed to the wheel to act as a brake

slack low ground (North of England)

snicket path between gardens (Lancs.)

spurway bridleway

stance grassy hollow on a drove road where cattle could rest and graze

stump-road road made of tree stumps

sumpter packhorse

swire a steep pass between mountains; a declivity; a hill road

tewer passage between fences or houses (Oxfordshire)

toll-bar turnpike

toll-booth town hall

toll-nook, tolsey, &c. place where market-tolls were taken

towling whipping horses up and down the road at a fair to show off their paces

trace track or path

tram a beam of timber; a road made of beams or logs (North of England)

trancite passage

tranter carrier (cf. Thomas Hardy's works)

trap two-wheeled carriage

trave a frame into which farriers put unruly horses

travers, travis a road crossing a highway

traverse the space outside a blacksmith's shop where horses were shod

trigen a skid-pad for a wheel

troacher a dealer in smuggled goods

trod, trode footpath, from trodden way

tumble-car an early form of cart in which the axle was fixed to the wheels and turned round with them

turbary the right to dig turf on another's land

twiss, twitch, twitchen, twitten a narrow alley

twizel fork of a river

unthank land held without the consent of the owner; a squatter holding

upping-stones mounting blocks

vennel alley (French)

want, went, weint, waylett place where two or more ways meet or cross

way Old English *weg*

waywarden surveyor of highways

whale isolated rounded hill (North of England)

whappleway bridleway

wash a lane through which water runs (East of England)

washman a beggar who solicits charity with sham sores

wath a ford (North of England)

waygate a gate across a road

whetstone given as an award to the person who told the biggest lie

whim the brow ot a hill (Dorset)

whirligig a turnstile; a carriage

widge-beasts wild Dartmoor and Exmoor ponies that were rounded up and driven into an enclosure through a fenced wedge (like a duck decoy in a river). The surname Widgery was given to the man in charge of the enclosure. Those who made it and drove the beasts were called Widgers

wynd alleyway; a narrow passage

Index